BACKSTORIES AND REVIEW QUOTES FOR THE BIRTH-FATHERS' CLUB SERIES

Backstory of *Finding Faith: The Birth-Fathers' Club Series*:

LIKE A TWISTING DOUBLE HELIX OF DNA, these two satisfying stories of compelling and complex father-daughter pairs entwine with life-altering surprises. They bring compassion, humor, and understanding to the question of whether it is ever too late for paternal instinct.

EACH YEAR THOUSANDS OF MEN father children later placed for adoption or donor-conception. Some of them thought they would forget. Some claim they never knew. There are several million of these secret fathers in the United States alone – in The Birth-Fathers' Club Series eight of them are about to get a knock on the door – as changing times catch up with them and with adoptive parents, recipient parents, anonymous donors, and the rest of our beloved ancestors.

Advanced Praise for *Finding Faith: The Birth-Fathers' Club Series*:

"USING HER DEFT STORYTELLING SKILLS, Michele Kriegman...instills complex...issues with emotional immediacy. We get to know the ensemble cast of characters and to care about them as if we were family.... *Finding Faith* has a strong, satisfying ending."

~ Elaine Durbach, former Bureau Chief, *NJ Jewish News*, author of the novel *Roundabout*

"VERY TOUCHING, THE ENDING FEELS SO AUTHENTIC.... Great story, and I enjoy all the connections Michele Kriegman makes between adoption and literature, the Bible, religion, poetry, plays, and more."

~ Traci Onders, Staff Search Specialist, Adult Adoptees & DNA Discoveries at Adoption Network, Cleveland

"IN *FINDING FAITH*, MS. KRIEGMAN IS MASTERFUL at capturing the tension and emotion of a reunion between newfound genetic relatives. Her characters come to life on the page, rendering the drama and trauma so familiar to the Misattributed Parent Experience (MPE) community. Join Faith and her loved ones on the tumultuous ride of a DNA surprise, the emotional fallout...and finally the potential for redemption."

~ Alesia Weiss, Co-founder, Right to Know

"MICHELE BRILLIANTLY CAPTURES THE NUANCES of search and reunion for both the biological family as well as the relinquished/ adopted person. Her characters have relatable, realistic internal dialogues about the inevitable tensions in reunion and discovery. Her prose in world building flows naturally and beautifully setting the scene while drawing the reader through the narrative."

~ Ridghaus, documentary film-maker of "Six Word Adoption Memoirs"

"THIS IS GREAT WRITING!... CALLS ON ALL FIVE senses.... Good suspense! As an adoptee who enjoyed ten years of reunion with my birth-father, it's wonderful to see the often under-represented and much needed birth-father perspectives Michele captures in *Finding Faith*."

~ Patricia Meyer, adoptee, advocate and blogger at My Adopted Life

"...THE OPPORTUNITY TO READ A STORY which brings together so many issues and conversations which arise from DNA discoveries....

This story is delivered with compassion and understanding for these characters based on the experiences of real people."

~ Fred Firestone, Misattributed Parentage Experience (MPE) community advocate

Backstory of *Tapioca Fire*, the 2014 prequel to *The Birth-Fathers' Club Series*:

TAPIOCA FIRE opens when Susan tries to solve the mystery of a missing parent only to uncover a greater crime. Susan was adopted years ago in Thailand. A once-in-a-lifetime career opportunity brings her to Japan for the opening of a new museum. It also gives her the excuse to hop another flight to visit the world of the woman forced to give her away years ago.

Susan's quest introduces her to the subculture of the adoption search and reunion movement. There is the detective Susan hires who specializes in adoption reunions and carries a secret of his own. Her journey rocks her marriage to David whose father abandoned the family years ago. Together they explore the rich spirituality behind David's decision not to pursue his own lost parent. Then that secret finds them.

But it is as much the story of her adoptive parents who were part of the pioneering generation who adopted internationally. They visit Thailand, a country of precious gems and orphans, convulsed by the struggles for democracy. They join the first generation to have their adult children return overseas to find birth family.

Her poignant meeting with her birth mother uncovers a deeper tragedy they will both begin to fight from their very different lives. Beautiful, dangerous, haunting, this quest is Susan's: she discovers the truth behind her relinquishment, sees the life she might have led, and finds a new purpose for her life going forward. *Tapioca Fire* proves the adage that the most difficult part of a quest is the journey back home.

Praise for *Tapioca Fire*, the 2014 prequel to *The Birth-Fathers' Club Series*:

"THIS WAS A BEAUTIFULLY WRITTEN work that held my interest and heart throughout.... Ms. Gilbert [Michele Kriegman]...makes you understand and relate easily to her characters.... I find myself quoting several very poignant, well-turned phrases even after finishing the book."
~ Iris J. Arenson-Fuller, PCC, CPC

"[T]HIS BOOK AND THE OTHERS IN HER *BIRTH-FATHERS' CLUB SERIES* remind me of another favorite writer, Amor Towles. Great reads that respect the reader's intelligence while moving a character-driven story with a good pace and populated by intriguing characters.

Tapioca Fire is one of those books that you start out reading for the themes--in this case, how people come to terms with losses such as being adopted or being abandoned by a parent--but it is so well-written that you quickly shift to reading it for the sheer pleasure of the reading itself.

The pacing, prose, and descriptions are that good.... it is clear that the author has thought deeply about and around the issues...she is able to present nuanced and deeply shaded stories and characters that are real and believable. I always like books like this where the author is able to distill her broad understanding of a person or topic into a concentrated package--called a book--so that the reader feels the larger echoes of the story....

Her sense of place is very strong.... her evocation of Thailand reads very true to me. Same can be said of her descriptions of rural Maine. A beautifully written book with vibrant real characters."
~ Mark Furman, The Tired Married Guys (TMG) Book Club

"WE ALL SEARCH FOR LOVE and acceptance.... [Michele Kriegman writing as] Suzanne Gilbert brings that struggle to life in a saga of a search and discovery that crosses continents and generations."
~ Elaine Durbach, former Bureau Chief, *NJ Jewish News*, author of *Roundabout*

"AS A THERAPIST WHO SPECIALIZES in adoption...I have recommended *Tapioca Fire* to my clients, and I would also recommend it to someone wanting a fascinating fiction read."

~ Brooke Randolph, LMHC

Backstory of *ROCK MEMOIR: Book 1 of The Birth-Fathers' Club Series*:

EVERY YEAR THOUSANDS OF MEN father children later placed for adoption or donor-conception. Some of them thought they would forget. Some claim they never knew. There are several million of these secret fathers in the United States alone-in The Birth-Fathers' Club Series eight of them are about to get a knock on the door. Tony Silvio, the detoxed but still howling Rock God epicenter of The Tony Silvio Project, is one of them. When his biological daughter finds him his rock memoir tour spins in a completely new orbit.

Praise for *ROCK MEMOIR: Book 1 of The Birth-Fathers' Club Series*:

"Michele Kriegman's novella, *ROCK MEMOIR*, is the first book in her *Birth Fathers' Club Series*, and it is a really fun way to kick off this series. The book tackles the serious topic of birth-fathers by using warmth, humor, and fast-paced writing. I especially found Tony, the aging rock idol, and his long-suffering wife, Maria, to be fascinating and alive.

The characters are well-realized and feel like people you may know--or think you know--and the story never gets bogged down by what could be a weighty subject--birth fathers who many years later start to deal with the fact that they have unknown children out there; and in some cases children they only recently became aware existed. Yet while the underlying theme is birth-fathers, the focus of this novella is squarely on character development and story line, making for a quick and enjoyable read.

Generally adoption-related books (fiction and memoir) are centered on what is called the "adoption triad"--adoptee, birth mother, and adopters. But there is a fourth actor who is almost always ignored or given short-shrift--the birth father. Their stories are equally as complex, varied, and compelling, as ROCK MEMOIR brings to life on the page"

~ Mark Furman, The Tired Married Guys (TMG) Book Club

Backstory of *From a Desert by the Sea: Book 2 of The Birth-Fathers' Club Series*:

ONE NIGHT TWO DISSIMILAR MEN, Clay Dennen, a North American family man and seasoned executive, and Ryuji Kato, the sharp-witted, executive producer of Japan's top morning show, meet in a seaside lounge and leave with the other's darkest secret. See how their stories ravel and recombine.

EVERY YEAR THOUSANDS OF MEN father children later placed for adoption or donor-conception. Some of them thought they would forget. Some claim they never knew. There are several million of these secret fathers in the United States alone-in The Birth-Fathers' Club Series eight of them are about to get a knock on the door.

Praise for *From a Desert by the Sea: Book 2 of The Birth-Fathers' Club Series*:

"The suspense of the search and DNA was intriguing...so haphazard at first then so coldly exacting in the end.... Michele has managed to weave secret adoption, reunion and the forgotten role of birth-fathers into a work of art that reads like a murder mystery. Archaic closed adoption laws lay the groundwork but love and the power of DNA steal the show."

~ MAJ Peter W. Franklin (Ret.) RPh, AdopteesWithOutLiberty.com /AWOL

"This captures it perfectly."

~ Michael Hering, father of two, parent of one

"[T]he story [is] engaging, the writing fluid...real characters."
~ Ridghaus, documentary film-maker of "Six Word Adoption Memoirs"

"AWESOME!"
~ Rob Manzanares, a father in "The Red Pill" documentary on men's rights

FINDING FAITH

Finding Faith

The Birth-Fathers' Club Series

A MEMOIRISH NOVEL BY

MICHELE KRIEGMAN

Reunion Land Press

REUNION LAND PRESS FIRST PRINTING, 2022

ISBN-978-1-7379477-4-5

Reunion Land Press

To my mother, Carolyn Margaret Kriegman, and my sister, Melisa Ann Hauben.

*And he shall turn the heart of the fathers to the children,
and the heart of the children to their fathers;*

~ Malachi, 3:24

CONTENTS

Timeline of The Birth-Fathers' Club Series
1

Prologue
3

Part 1

~ 1 ~
Solomon 2024, Florida, Republic of Vietnam & New York
City
7

~ 2 ~
Faith
26

Part 2

~ 3 ~
Bill 2022, New York City
67

~ 4 ~

Faith 2022, New York City & New Jersey

75

~ 5 ~

Susan 2023, New Jersey

88

~ 6 ~

Faith 2023, New Jersey

100

~ 7 ~

Susan 2023, New York City & New Jersey

104

~ 8 ~

Solomon 2024, Florida

114

Part 3

~ 9 ~

Bill 2022, New York City

128

~ 10 ~

Faith 2022, London & New Jersey

140

~ 11 ~
Bill 2022, New York City
144

~ 12 ~
Faith 2022, New Jersey
159

~ 13 ~
Bill 2023, New York City
166

Part 4

~ 14 ~
Susan 2023, New York City
170

~ 15 ~
Faith 2023, New Jersey
176

~ 16 ~
Bill 2023, New York City
186

~ 17 ~
Faith 2024, New Jersey
211

Part 5

~ 18 ~

Susan 2024, Florida

222

~ 19 ~

Solomon 2024, Florida

225

~ 20 ~

Faith 2025, New York City

233

~ 21 ~

Bill 2025, New York City

239

~ 22 ~

Finding Faith

241

Reading Club Discussion 1: Soundtrack For The Documentary

252

Reading Club Discussion 2: Quiz By Faith, "Is It Redemption Or Is It Absurdity?"

254

ACKNOWLEDGEMENTS - 259
ABOUT THE AUTHOR - 261

TIMELINE OF THE BIRTH-FATHERS' CLUB SERIES

1970 – Like other Black, Jewish, Latino, and Native American servicemen who performed acts of heroism in Vietnam worthy of the US Congressional Medal of Honor or Distinguished Service Cross, Sgt. First Class Solomon L. Morris is overlooked.

1972 – A US couple adopts a toddler, Susan, from a maternity home/orphanage on the outskirts of Bangkok; Faith is born and relinquished as rates of single motherhood rise; and, the US Supreme Court legalizes birth control.

1973 – Abortion becomes legal in the US.

1975 – "Baby Dennen" is born and relinquished.

1978 – The first "test-tube baby" is born; Congress passes the Indian Child Welfare Act (the ICWA).

1989 – The Tony Silvio Project plays a concert in Boise, Idaho.

2007 – Dan is adopted from Guatemala by Jim and Samantha.

2009 – Run-DMC rapper Darryl McDaniels testifies in Trenton, NJ for heritage equality.

2011-12 – Faith and Susan attend grad school in Japan; Mormons launch mass market DNA testing.

2019 – Faith gets the first phone call from her birth-mother and connects with Susan at the Adoption Triad Circle. Former president of Peru, Alberto Fujimori, is extradited from Japan; Ryuji Kato and Clay Dennen meet.

2020 – Ted seeks birth-fathers and donors to testify for adoptee and donor-conceived people (DCP) heritage equality.

1

2021 – Tony Silvio kicks off The Tony Silvio Project Backstories World Tour and the book tour for his memoir. Dan faces becoming a birth-father himself.

2022 – Bill reveals secrets before Faith flies to meet her birth-mother. A search angel army helps Clay.

2023 – Susan and Faith take DNA tests. Anita attacks adoptees and DCPs.

2024 – Bill sees adoptees and DCPs support Faith in a bittersweet discovery. Two phone calls change everything for Master Sergeant Solomon L. Morris, US Army (Ret). Baoyu, one of over a quarter of a million Chinese birth-fathers, is found by his daughter.

2025 – Clay delivers a letter to Faith.

2021 – **FF DOCUMENTARY** – Ryuji and Faith kick off pre-production work; Tony Silvio meets backstage with Clay and Dan.

2024 – **FF DOCUMENTARY** – After travel and courthouse delays, filming kicks off in New York, Tokyo, and Washington, D.C.

2025 – **FF DOCUMENTARY** – Post-production, Faith negotiates concert footage; Ryuji distributes *The Birth-Fathers' Club* globally.

PROLOGUE

Faith checked the English language closed captioning that ran a beat behind the Japanese voiceover on the overhead. She was the only one in the production studio at 1 AM who understood both languages:

"A year ago, Rock & Roll Hall of Famer Tony Silvio of the Tony Silvio Project struck an unlikely partnership with Fortune 500's Clay Dennen in a class action lawsuit brought by Park Avenue attorney-to-the-oligarchs Ted Landtsman. Now trace the international movement their 'Birth-Fathers Club' awakened through the award-winning investigation produced by Fuji-Hoshizora Media's own Ryuji Kato. Streaming at 11."

Her boss, Ryuji Kato, asked her to confirm a date onscreen with filming notes in the binder. She flipped open the binder. He'd insisted on nicknaming the binder "Finding Faith" – she quickly shortened that to FF. The FF binder detailed scene descriptions/dialogue for reenactments, contained storyboards mapping out all five parts of the documentary, and labelled each section with the approximate date and one of the documentary's four points of view. Every documentary section opened with Faith, Solomon, and Susan looking straight into the camera, each answering the same interview question from their point of view.

More than four years of work and delays, but here it was. In less than twenty-four hours the story of the Birth-Fathers' Club was going to be seen around the world.

Part 1

Excerpts from the FF documentary:

FAITH

"'What do I realize I *already* had *before* I began my quest?' Kind of like the Wizard of Oz where adoptee Dorothy already had a home, the tinman already had a heart, and the scarecrow already had brains, isn't it? Well, even before I located my birth-father, I found my tribe when I found other adult adoptees and donor-conceived people."

SOLOMON

"'Are birth-fathers trying to redeem themselves through testifying for the rights of adoptees and donor-conceived people?' Hmm, I didn't know the girl became pregnant, nor was the context one of a relationship. But as soon as I did know my child was looking for me, I acknowledged her. Hmm, redemption? I strive to be a quiet professional as we say in the Green Berets. I try to live my daily life right: yielding in traffic, paying my taxes, and choosing to join a congregation even though I have my reasonable doubts. Once I was asked, yes, testifying became part of all that."

SUSAN

"'What do I realize I *already* had *before* I began my quest?' I already have an adoptive family I love and my own family I love raising. Museum curating is work that I love and my sense of history and connection to something larger than myself comes from that. But it feels good to see birth-fathers in the Birth-Fathers' Club fighting for us."

~ 1 ~

SOLOMON 2024, FLORIDA, REPUBLIC OF VIETNAM & NEW YORK CITY

I was born Solomon Leonard Morris in Tulsa, Oklahoma and was raised and married at B'nai Israel Temple, although that ended and I've lived for years with just me, myself, and dog. First came Chamomile. She was a chocolate lab who developed bad hips and on one of the saddest days of my life she had to be put down. Then there were the twins, two yappy white poodles that my eldest niece left with me when she went to live in Madrid for a year that kept extending itself until it was evident to everyone that Winston and Chester were mine, despite my protests that they weren't real dogs. They both lived to a good old age but I found myself having to walk them four times a day by the end. Suited me just fine as I'd just moved to Florida around that time and the walks got me familiar with the neighbors in the development.

Next, and maybe finally, is Shotgun, another lab, a

black lab who likes to ride shotgun with me, window down, along the flat open roads of south Florida.

Then one day I get a call from a dark night of my past, a war I'd closed the door on.

I find myself going through it all again.

I was one of the first Green Berets consigned by President John F. Kennedy. On May twenty-first, nineteen sixty-nine in Ap Tan Hoa, Vietnam I led soldiers across enemy lines to retrieve my platoon leader. It turned out he had been killed. I went a little crazy—that's what it must have looked like to the rest of the men. I was as clear headed as can be. Not a wasted motion. I single-handedly destroyed enemy forces hidden in bunkers that had pinned down our battalion, but I got shot three times.

In the war I learned to plan, and I learned to expect the unexpected. If *this* isn't the first goddamn out of the blue bolt that ever hit me since then, it's surely the biggest one. And I reacted on my feet. The reaction was the right one.

I, Sol Morris, get a voicemail from a stranger who introduces himself as Clarence Dennen. The voice explains cheerfully that he "served in a tin can in Nam". I haven't heard that term for a destroyer in years. The message is short and ends with, "We've got something else in common that may come as a surprise. Please call me back as soon as possible."

When I do get back to him, Clay doesn't waste much time. Seems he is the volunteer leader of a group of former military who are working to do right. *Working to do right?*

Clay explains he's begun helping GIs and their children reunite. Then Clay gets to the chase, "We both fathered children when we were in uniform."

I don't remember what I said, probably mumbled something to Clay about being stunned. I also don't believe it but I *do* believe something about him. I am still trying to let the news of a child sink in when Clay adds that he has been volunteering to help my daughter, Susan, find me. *My daughter!* She was raised by a nice American couple here stateside and would be calling me herself shortly. Clay went on that the girl had, on her own, spoken to one of my distant cousins back in Oklahoma.

How come no one called to tell me? My sister would have.

Clay seemed to have read my mind because immediately he said, "Susan contacted a cousin who came up as a DNA match. The woman didn't seem to want to check into things more. That, and Susan's birth-mother not being sure of your name made Susan reach out to me. This left us with you, as well as two other male cousins, both the right age."

Is this really happening? I have a healthy skepticism and two questions come to mind. "Sure must be interesting stuff, these new DNA tests. But how accurate are they? You hear all the time with medical tests about false positives or false negatives," I point out.

"For parent-child results it's one-hundred percent accurate. There are areas where the tests are not one-hundred percent accurate: beyond fourth cousins for certain ethnic groups, say, it may show you being closer to a cousin than you really are. For genetic diseases it can only show that you may have the gene but depending on the gene, it may need something else to happen – epigenetics – or the presence of another particular set of genes for it to actually show up as the illness. Even for ethnicities it can vary because a kit will look for only some ethnic markers but it's not as accurate as a full, expensive genome mapping. But, for parent-child results? There are no false positives or false negatives," said Clay.

I ask, "So you tracked it to me without me even taking a test? Maybe that cousin you reached was the guy you're looking for..."

"Listen, I agree you don't know me from Adam," said Clay, "You're only going to have peace of mind if you take the test yourself. We used AncestrologyDNA. Set up your own account without me or Susan involved at all. You buy a kit, spit in a tube and send it back in their postage-paid box. The results show up on an account you set up on their website. Only you handle the results and I won't be involved. For close family like you and Susan, the results are one-hundred percent, and you'll see for yourself what they are."

"No disrespect, I may just do that," said Sol. Clay is likable enough but the odds that I have a kid I don't know about are probably a lot less than the odds of someone running a telephone scam.

"None taken. We use Ancestrology because they have the largest database. But even before you check this out on your own, I can tell you how we narrowed it down," said Clay.

"That was my second question. Why me and not the two other cousins?" I ask.

"You have a male cousin who served in the army and took an AncestrologyDNA test but he's more distant than a father or even an uncle, meaning shares fewer segments and centimorgans with Susan."

"Do I need to understand 'segments' and 'centimorgans' for this?" I ask.

"Not at all, Solomon," said Clay.

"Sol."

"Sol. The other cousin, he was the right age but he had a desk job stateside during the war and didn't take a DNA test. If he'd been sent over, I'd be calling him too. I prefer not to call family if I can rule them out by geography like this. It's really between a serviceman and his child," said Clay.

A serviceman and his child...

Clay is still speaking, "...Susan is healthy, married, employed and raising three kids, a daughter and twins, boy and girl."

"That's just great," I say, or something to that effect. We talk for a while. I am trying to figure out a place for everything Clay has just told me. I go silent but my mind is racing. He tells me that he'll give her my number, that it's important to let the adoptee take charge. I think I agree, not that he is asking my permission.

I fathered a child over there on leave?

It was a girl, grown now. She is stateside and looking for me?

How did she get here? One of those orphan airlifts?

Raised by an American couple so she must speak English. That's a relief.

How do I know this isn't some kind of scam? I didn't have much opportunity to fraternize, as they called it.

The exception was that one little sing-song girl I picked up in Thailand. I went there on a leave they'd given me right after my platoon leader was killed.

If this is some kind of hoax, I'm sure I can stay sharp and suss it out quickly. If this Susan really is my child, I wonder what I owe her. What does she want?

Clay breaks the silence to remind me that Susan isn't asking anything for herself. Then he tells me something else...

"The two of us, we're both what you call 'birth-fathers'."

"'Birth-father'," I say, trying it out. I check my watch because I have to go out again to meet someone for racquet ball.

"Welcome to the club," Clay says before we both hang up.

* * *

I get home from racquet ball and lower myself and my throbbing knees into an easy chair. The light is flashing on the phone again. I mop my forehead with a terry cloth and then put it on the end table before reaching for the handset.

I wonder if this message is going to be that Clay again. I take a sip from my water bottle and press the button for the message. I don't recognize the woman's voice. It must be her.

I play it twice.

She said her American name was "Susan Piper" but that her birth-name... I've never heard the term "birth-name" ...is *Suwan*. Doesn't ring a bell.

Susan mentions Phuket and pronounces it correctly, POO-ket, then calls it a resort island. But when I visited, it was a spit of wild tropics wreathed in white sand and aqua reef.

She mentions the year she was born. Then it adds up.

She mentions her birth-mother's name: "Noklek". I think I may have heard it. I believe Susan all right but I'll keep my common sense as this plays out.

I copy down her name and number but feel like calling *this instant* to get it over with. On the other hand, I still haven't shed these sweaty clothes from racquet ball, so I heave myself out of the recliner and amble down the hall to the shower.

I am dressed and still toweling my hair as I go to the kitchen. I place the slip of paper with her number on the dinette, rummage in a cabinet and pull out a can of soup. Nothing beats salty after a good game.

Clearly, this has been a project for that old sea dog

named Clay and this lady he is helping, Susan. Did they yell, "Eureka!" when they found me?

I haven't been looking for anything.

While Clay and Susan may have made their destination by finding me – I laugh at the thought that I might be anyone's holy grail – for me this is like King Arthur pulling the sword from the stone. That was the sign that Arthur will be king. The sword wasn't the destination, it wasn't a holy grail. It was the call to begin the quest.

I am sure this is the beginning of something. I'm just not sure what it means I am called to do.

Then another thought occurs to me. Are they hunting me down for child support? I've heard of something like this. I suppose it's the right thing for me to do. I have no other children.... The world is beginning to shift; I have a child. But she's also someone else's child.

During the war I knew that some men—American, French, or Vietnamese over in Laos and Cambodia—kept local girls as "war wives". Very few brought them back as "war brides" though. Right or wrong, you put these sing-song girls in a separate category. Most other dog-faces didn't do too much philosophizing and therefore didn't question paying for their services. Hell, a grenade, direct mortar fire, even an old landmine from the French occupation could take you out in a heartbeat. This might be the last woman you'd ever be with. Carpe diem, seize the day.

Now this young woman said her birth-mother's name is Noklek and that does ring a bell. I picked her up in Bangkok or somewhere near the base. There wasn't much to say about the arrangement with the sing-song girl. I got a jeep and went to one of those fishbowls where you go to hire a "short-term girlfriend". The fishbowl was a store window in front of rows of girls sitting on risers. The guys in the barracks told me to go early in the morning because the girls were like berries. Go early and the best hadn't been plucked but go late and they all looked wilted, bored.

Her hair and eyes were especially black and shiny. Something angular about her collar bone, her arms. That wasn't something you could share with a young adoptee in regards to her mother. My mind hits a blank wall.

At any rate, we were together for most of my leave which I used to go visit – wait for it – a newly completed civil engineering project called the Sarasin Bridge. Getting clear across Thailand with a prostitute as a guide wasn't your typical choice for leave, especially to see a civil engineering project. Back then that kind of construction, in and of itself an elegant creation, seemed to hold so much hope amidst all the poverty. There was already a regional air strip on the mainland side of the Andaman Sea and a few rowers had set up a ferry. But I only wanted to see Phuket by the newly opened Sarasin Bridge that this girl and I could now take to get there.

* * *

King Arthur built a round table, brought knights

together in a just and fair Camelot. How did that translate? I should get to know Susan's kids? If she even wants that.

Susan spoke to a distant cousin. Who? Should I introduce her to my sister's family? After all, my nieces and nephews are biologically her first cousins.

I have no idea how my sister will take all this. Will she welcome this Susan as a new niece? She is getting crankier about change. I don't know.

This young lady—I will call her that but I can't call her a daughter—I don't see what I have to offer her.

I look again at the number I took down while listening to Clay's voicemail. For a nostalgic moment three songs skitter in from old Billboard charts: Tommy Tutone's "867-5309 / Jenny" from forty years ago, then Glenn Miller's "Pennsylvania 6-5000," and right before my first tour in 'Nam, "Beechwood 4-5789" written by Marvin Gaye performed by the Marvelettes. *Whatever happened to them?*

I let myself whistle a few bars before putting down the piece of paper with the girl's message and call my sister Yitzie instead.

By the end of the call, one hour and forty-five minutes long, I'm feeling pretty good, even sentimental. She's caught me up on the rest of the clan. Count on my sister to provide the verbiage that never occurs to me: questions to ask, sharing about Uncle Ned dropping suddenly in his forties from a heart condition no one suspected – that's the kind of thing they'd want on medical histories for her or her children – and, what to call Susan.

"Why not just 'Susan'?" I say.

"No, that's not what I mean, Sollie. Are you going to call her your 'biological daughter'? Sollie, you need some kind of adjective –"

"You mean something from a series about Vikings like 'his bastard son' or 'their changeling daughter'? Nah, I think I better stay away from those adjectives –"

"You can't just be her father and she can't just be your daughter because she already has a father and mother."

I consider what Yitzie says for a minute before laughing out loud, "I think I already fought this fight with Ma when you were born. I tried to convince her to take you back to the hospital because she already had a child: me!"

"Sollie!"

"So, I'll tell you now what Ma told me then," I say, explaining it to her straight-faced, "Ma had enough love for more than one child. Ma would always love me even with you, the new baby, horning in. I imagine Susan has enough room to love more than one set of parents. And she will always love the mother and father who raised her."

"You know, that makes sense."

If I'd offered to let her, Yitzie would have called the girl herself. We laugh and promise to speak again soon.

I take a circuit again down the hall, through the Florida room and the bedroom before stopping in the den to pass each of the framed photos: My platoon. Headquarters. A hunting party in Pennsylvania.

An old beret hangs from a peg. I rotate it to help it keep its shape.

To no one in particular and to each of the faces on the

wall I say, "It's time." Then I reach down to take the desk phone from its cradle.

* * *

I make the right decision, the honorable one, and I agree to meet in New York City—in a public place, of course. Suddenly the world is smaller, in a good way. A clean, well-lighted place, as they say. I'm laughing with something like relief, I guess. And excitement.

So that's all there is to it?

Not exactly. I do order and take a DNA test but it will take a while before I get the results. I let Susan know that, figuring she'll cancel if she's not the real deal.

I fly north later that same week to visit my nieces and nephews in Oklahoma, then drive a rental car all the way east, cross the George Washington Bridge over the Hudson River into New York City, and then take an avenue south to find parking and meet her at a coffee shop in Manhattan. She picked it out.

When I walk in and scan the room I see—a young woman—waiting by a booth in the back. Normal height. Long, brown-black hair. The booth, the walls, and the narrow hanging lamps are all oranges and browns. I walk straight toward her and her face comes into focus in the warm glow of a lamp. The bridge of her nose gracefully flattening into wide, dark, delicately lidded eyes. Medium complexion that could also be Latina or Mediterranean but she happens to be half southeast Asian from her mother.

Incredibly normal. I sit down, a waiter takes our orders and we begin to talk. I swig the ice water. One of the bus boys dressed in black with a short black apron pivots on the waxed floor and I only notice because his black shoes squeak in the still quiet late-morning as he to goes retrieve a water pitcher. I didn't drink enough on the last leg of the drive this morning.

I'm still sucking on a sliver of ice as I take in the way Susan tilts her head slightly as she listens, or her modulated voice, subdued gestures, and a twinkle that hints at more of a sense of humor once we both get to know each other better.

I get up for a pair of salt and pepper shakers over on the white marble counter. She's watching me and I know I walk like an ex-marine or an ex-cop. We didn't hug the moment we met like some television reunion. Ten years after retirement and even with letting my crew cut grow I'm still spotted as former military.

Susan. I see the shared dimple and curved lips that make merriment merrier on us. Honestly, I can only remember a little of this young woman's mother though. Her graceful hands are her mother's. Birth-mother's.

Thank goodness she hasn't inherited my bear of a frame. I have a thick neck and a barrel chest but they say I haven't lost the spring in my step that always kept me light on my feet. Her frame is lithe and liquid like an otter. Her voice is pitched like any other stateside girl's. I remember faintly the sing-song drawl of the petite evening lady I took with me on leave all those years ago. It just occurs to me now that the high pitch of the Thai girl's voice could have been an affectation. Probably "sing-song girl" is a term you don't use anymore, although it's sweet. "Sex worker"? That sounds hard to me, more aggressive than I remember her with her lilting voice and gentle ways. I guess her occupation doesn't change a thing about her being Susan's first mother.

When the coffee arrives, I notice there's something familiar about Susan's fingers, how she holds the mug like everyone in my family. She pulls out photos from her bag. A husband, three children, the younger two twins, like she told me on the phone. I should be more interested than I am but they're not real yet. She doesn't seem to realize how full my senses are just getting used to the reality of her. There is no need to rush for the photographs to fill the silence. I guess she's as nervous as I'm realizing I am.

Still, I'm guarded, no harm in that. I find I am answering questions. I guess I owe her that. What runs in the family? How long did they live? I always took this intel for granted.

Then she asks, "Tell me about your birth."

That one startles me. Of course, I know the answer though no one has ever asked me the question before. I've always known the story, can't remember when I learned it, just grew up with it. It occurs to me that she, like other adoptees, is coming at life from a different direction. Of course she wouldn't know the details of her birth. I tell her what I can of mine.

"How were you raised?" she asks earnestly. *An American question if ever there is one in this mosaic land.*

"Jewish. My mother was the pious one. Dad only liked the schnapps with the other men after services."

"So, you were affiliated? Which one?"

I laugh. She knows the lingo of the tribe, this eager Amerasian stranger so, I surmise, her adoptive parents or husband must be Jewish too. We can connect over these community memories even though we didn't share them together. If her adoptive parents celebrated Christmas or Easter, we could trade stories about them too.

Holidays are not too personal like a birthday. A birthday might be the anniversary of her relinquishment.

"Conservative," I answer, "Back then it was really what nowadays you'd call Conservadox, midway between Conservative and Orthodox. No women at the pulpit but couples could sit together."

"We were Reform," Susan says, "No schnapps out of respect for people in recovery. Except on Purim."

"Ah, Purim. I remember one year my dad agreed to buy a tri-cornered hat to dress me up as Haman, you know, the villain who wants to manipulate the king into killing Princess Esther and her Uncle Mordechai?"

"Yes, and all the rest of the Jews of Persia," she laughs, "so did he buy you the tri-cornered hat to be Haman?"

"Yes, ma'am, but with one condition: I had to promise to use it again in another ten months for a Halloween costume."

"So, with that hat, you went as a continental soldier for Halloween?"

"No, a pirate."

Susan laughs an "aaaaargh", then asks, "We used to have a circus company inflate a bouncy house inside the social hall. The teenagers set up a midway with bean tosses and tickets and prizes for the Sunday school."

"Mm-hmm. Did you have a play about the Book of Esther?" I ask.

"A *purimshpiel*? Yes."

"You know what that is?" More is coming back to me about the Purim traditions. I am enjoying this and add, "And our parents let us write 'Haman' or 'Amalek' on the bottom of our Sabbath shoes so we could erase their names."

Susan joins back with, "Oh, yeah, we'd write Haman's name on the bottom of our sneakers and stomp whenever they read his name from the Torah. To stamp it out.

"Did you boo?" I ask.

"Booed, stamped our feet, and swung those noisemakers, um, *groggers,* whenever we heard their names." Susan asks, "Did you have carnations?"

"No, never heard of that," I tell her.

"We had baskets just inside the sanctuary filled with white carnations. You were supposed to take one and bring it to your pew. Then whenever they read Queen Esther's name from the *megillah*, you were supposed to wave the flower and say 'aaah'."

It is coming back to me, the annual Purim carnival that arrived around the time of an Oklahoma thaw. There was an old beatnik who used to show up on his Harley, a corner of Ginsberg's *Kaddish* sticking out of his leather jacket. He brought a large bottle of vodka and Dixie cups with him. He'd walk up and down the aisles of the sanctuary offering the adults shots. In the front of the room a half dozen or so congregants leaned over the scroll of scripture, chanting the familiar Bible story in Hebrew.

"Guess what I was," she says breaking my reverie.

I must have grinned, "Esther. Every little girl was Queen Esther."

The boys had more choices to be one of the three male protagonists: treacherous Haman, foolish King Ahasuerus, or wise Uncle Mordechai. But all the girls chose to be Queen Esther who won the king's heart and saved the Jewish people. Each little Queen Esther wore a crown with either a long Middle Eastern tunic or Western ball gown that would reappear in ten months' time on Halloween - All Soul's Eve - as Cleopatra, Rapunzel or Cinderella.

Suddenly Susan asks, "How many birth-uncles and birth-aunts do I have?"

Strange term. She means my siblings.

Then she says something with a mild chastising tone "...any questions about me?" She delivers it with her head tilted in that way I can only describe as somehow familiar.

She is reminding me, probably, that I am being rude. I realize she's been asking the questions and I haven't asked her a single one about her.

She was the one who came looking. A month ago, she didn't even exist for me. That isn't all of it. Another part is that it's my natural tendency to stand back and just observe.

"Oh, I have a lot of questions," I lie, but my too long silence is a tell.

Susan smiles at me patiently. Eventually we make small talk for a few more minutes, me even adding a few questions. I am curious about her all right. I can just stare at her if I let myself. I don't really care personally about the answers to any of her questions; I'm not curious that way. I am curious in the way of dogs or seasoned poker players who learn everything they need to know by their senses. The smell of fresh air haloed her hair; Susan must have chosen to walk some ways to this restaurant. Her breath is faint, no tobacco nor last night's garlic, but I pick up the scent of her breathe and skin anyway and it is somehow comfortable at this small table. She smells young, she moves happy, she sounds engaged.

Touch is forbidden. More so with this first meeting than on a first date, less than with a business colleague. It seems neither of us are predisposed temperamentally to greet with hugs anyway. That said, when we get up at the end of the meal, I reach around her swiftly to get her coat from the old-fashioned coat hook. My knuckles, folded over her collar, brush her shoulders as she slides an arm into each sleeve. It isn't specific enough to be fatherly, just chivalrous: what well-raised men do. Instead, we bump arms as we walk out the door together. Neither of us flinches. It reminds us both that she is a good foot or so shorter than me: my daughter.

I paid for the tab and now offer to pay for a cab.

She points out, "You didn't even ask where I'm going."

"Where are you going?"

"Right around the corner. That's where our offices are."

We both pause. I wonder what rule applies here. The man offers to call a woman? Or, the professor never calls the student? More like the latter. She hesitates and gives me, I guess, a searching look.

So, I say, "Be in touch," and then add "Take care of yourself."

I am hesitant to walk away first because of that look—and it somehow seems wrong symbolically—so I watch her back thread through the crowds of that long avenue. If such a thing were possible, I wish a blessing, a benediction on her lustrous hair.

I am also watching for my own pleasure now, wondering who I can tell all this to. I am thinking, "It's not a romantic thing, but I'm drawn in. I am smitten. So this is flesh of my flesh."

~ 2 ~

FAITH

Her kind demeanor and book-strong habits helped Faith parlay a field producer role at the ABC News' Boston affiliate, then a journalism scholarship and friends' recommendations, into a job at the Tokyo Bureau of ABC News. She worked as the overnight desk editor, a shift that began with rounding up news reports from all the East Asian news bureaus and stringers, if they were on assignment, then relaying the news to the World Desk in New York where it was already morning due to the time difference.

Juggling this with graduate studies became her drug or her adventure, depending on how you looked at it. It found Faith walking up the hills of the Shibuya neighborhood after a day of classes to push the elevator button in one of the few high rises in this section of Tokyo. On a clear evening you could see all the way to Mount Fuji from the window of the overnight desk.

Another part of her job was to follow the news on all the major Japanese networks and translate the stories that were newsworthy for a North American audience. You couldn't help but notice how Japanese broadcasters emphasized different news stories from the desk back in New York. More on East Asia and less on Latin America here. Geography was only one piece of it. Producers also gave the Japanese audience more stories on science and technology breakthroughs.

A few staff would hang out with her during the early evening news but most crews and editors were packing up and leaving within half an hour of her arrival. Her then-boyfriend worked for public television not too far away and sometimes managed to swing by on his way to the train. But mostly it was her and a seasoned newsman named Ken. He was the cameraman for the Tokyo bureau, a Cambodian ex-pat who had lost a leg to a landmine. She wasn't sure if Ken was his real name or if he was using it because it was easy for both Japanese and English-speakers to say.

One evening, Ken and Faith were finishing the office pot of tea, and one of those technology breakthrough stories came on. Two graduates of Brigham Young had already digitized the Mormon Church's databases and were putting them online. The Church of Latter-Day Saints was, as most journalists knew, an excellent source for tracking down the life profile of a deceased person. They kept baptismal records, social security death benefits, immigration records, you name it. The Mormons were the go-to since at least the late '90s but now, according to the Japanese television report, the two entrepreneurs would soon be offering "DNA testing".

Ken sat up straighter, "Can you picture the revolution for us someday? For diasporas like Cambodians, for immigrants?"

"For something large scale like a diaspora, if they can build up a large enough database of names to connect people, it'll be great. Wait – I missed the name. AncestrologyDNA or something like that?"

Then they dropped the topic and the conversation drifted to the next news story. Back then it didn't occur to Faith, an adoptee, that adoptees or donor-conceived people would ever look for their heritage, that they had the same right to it as anyone else.

* * *

One time when they were alone in the office, Ken finishing up and she just beginning her shift, an earthquake rocked the walls and floor.

She must have cried out because he came out of his office.

"Stand with your feet wider apart."

Faith followed his instructions but wondered what good it would do if the whole building came crashing down, "The floor is swaying and we're many floors above pavement."

"That's good," he said, "earthquake tolerant high rises are supposed to sway instead of buckle."

It was a lesson another American, Susan, was learning at about the same time on the other side of Tokyo. Both were graduate students, Susan in fine arts, and were destined to meet eight years in the future an hour outside New York City in a suburban county seat.

>>> 2019, NEW YORK, NEW JERSEY & LONDON

Faith and Susan finally met for the first time here in the large conference room of a public library an hour outside downtown Manhattan. Close to forty people sat in two concentric rings around a conference table as part of the monthly Adoption Triad Circle the first Monday night of the month. Now that adoptees were coming out of the closet of secrecy, they borrowed from other grassroots movements when they called it "coming out" or "being in reunion". This group, the ATC for short, was a self-help group for members of the adoption "triad" – adopted people, people who adopted, and people who placed their child for adoption – when they searched for separated relatives. Faith and Susan tried to show up monthly at the ATC.

Today Faith and Susan took a numbered ticket at the

door and managed to grab chairs at the inside circle right at the table.

Susan was a kindred spirit in some ways. When Faith and she realized during a break that they both worked in the city, spoke Japanese, and were raised with a Jewish adoptive parent, they had to get to know each other better. They liked to joke that they would have been twins— if Faith had been born petite, Eurasian and in Thailand, or if Susan had been a freckled, White kid with auburn hair born in New York City, raised in the 'burbs.

Instead, it was Faith who came from one of the "bridge and tunnel" suburbs garlanding the islands, peninsulas, and harbors of New York City. She was working as a local hire for a Japanese media network. Hoshizora-Fuji Media's bread and butter was a weekly segment Faith produced for the leading commercial Japanese morning show. She also she took on special assignments.

The older Japanese men at the network still needed a whole intro from her boss, Ryuji Kato, when another race or gender was being considered to staff a show, even *nisei,* ethnic Japanese Americans, whose only tribe difference was nationality. Ryuji would explain that her name "faith" means *shinkou* in Japanese. It made them feel more comfortable somehow about working with a foreigner. Even though she was an American and a woman, Ryuji and the local team allowed her eventually to produce the New York portion of their morning show, just the same as the Japanese staff, which was a first.

Faith knew Ryuji was proud to be this lit. Unlike most of Japanese corporate culture, the television industry attracted lone wolves and loose cannons who liked to explore the edges of society and behavior. Faith didn't forget for a minute how lucky she was to be accepted among them and managed the colleagues who were sometimes prone to wild energy and emotional outbursts with true fondness and respect.

But, as Faith admitted to Susan once, she could spin that same story from a completely different angle. Looking back, Faith recognized the salves and decisions that let her grow, even before "coming out" or "being in reunion". *I did what I didn't know I needed to do, Susan: create a blood connection to the world by becoming the first person in my college class to get married and the second to have a baby – before I went on to broadcast journalism. It took my late friend, Martha Woodroof, who followed the same "career path" from a Seven Sisters college to motherhood to NPR, to convince me I'm not a failure although rushing home to pick kids up from daycare seemed to be slowing – understatement – my ability to network in television.*

Her friend Susan's story was a little different. She came, as Susan put it, apparently out of thin air from Bangkok, Thailand where her White parents found her on a gem trading trip for a relative's business in Midtown New York's Diamond District. Susan's adoptive parents made that trip for the family gem business but included an afternoon at an orphanage. Susan called it thin air because she really knew nothing about her past or why she was given away. Adding to the mystery was that she was Amerasian with no information whatsoever about her paternal side and not much more about her maternal side.

Susan's adoptive dad liked to say they "came home with a sleeve of rubies and one bundle of doe-eyed daughter – the latter being the true treasure."

It was a phone call from a stranger that first drove Faith to seek out the Adoption Triad Circle where she first met Susan. Faith asked Susan if they could meet for lunch on a Friday and Susan agreed. Faith hoped Susan might become a kind of mentor because Susan was already "in reunion" with her birth-mother, as Faith hoped to be.

They chose a downstairs Japanese *yaki-tori* shop and ordered *a la carte* dishes from a traditional menu on polished wooden plaques with black brushstrokes on three of the four walls of the tiny eatery. It was half-way between Faith's office and the gallery where Susan was working as a curator for hire. Less than a year ago, Susan shared at the ATC, that she oversaw the finishing touches on a well-publicized museum opening in Nikko, Japan. Nikko was the city that brought the world "see no evil, hear no evil, speak no evil" through the delicately carved monkeys that adorned the eaves of a mountain shrine there. Right after the adrenaline high of the opening, Susan piled on more by heading to her birth-country for the very first time as an adult.

"Self-care," Susan told Faith at their lunch today, explaining her reason for the trip and for reaching out to adoptees and donor-conceived people.

Self-care? Maybe, thought Faith. But she thought she had a better sense of Susan. Was it only "self-care" and not the existence of a mystery, the promise of intrigue that drove her as much as it drove Faith?

What Faith did know about her own ancestry up to now had come through an innocent visit to her adoption agency for "non-identifying information". She just wanted to see what her adoption files might hold in the way of medical history. She knew her birth-mother's ethnicity matched her adoptive dad's and that there was nothing about her paternal heritage. Like Susan, Faith was raised with Jewish adoptive parents.

The files contained two revelations that came at her like rogue waves, capsizing her sense of identity, something that was hard to explain to most people.

She would still give it a try with Susan. The first surge was that the files, all along, had contained information about Faith's birth-father. The social worker explained that Faith's adoptive parents most likely did not have this information either and that's why Faith grew up being told no information existed.

Faith shifted uncomfortably as the social worker continued that, "pursuant to the Indian Child Welfare Act of 1978, adoption agency policy has changed, and we now have to reveal that your birth-father was of American Indian descent."

"If you knew, why didn't you tell my parents?" Faith asked.

"At the time," the social worker replied carefully, "it

was viewed as in everyone's best interest that they be 'given a fresh start.'"

Fresh start from what? Best interest for whom?

Almost as an afterthought, the social worker added that today their agency would have tried to place her with her birth-father's family, then after that with a family from the same tribe or at least with Indigenous prospective adoptive parents. Before 1978 the priority was a "fresh start".

There it is again. This social worker didn't use that language for my birth-mother or her ethnicity. Instead, the notes she read Faith about her birth-mother said something like "collegiate type". Faith's head was pounding.

Was this the language of the Indian residential schools where so many children died? Was this the language of the Indian Adoption Projects through which so many young children disappeared from their tribal culture?

She felt a growing horror. *I grew up knowing my adoptive parents' heritages but not my own. I grew up knowing my birth-mother's heritage, which matches my adoptive father's. My parents even made a point of it. I stopped wondering about my birth-father and my paternal heritage. So this is what the 19th century so-called "kill the Indian, save the child" policy became in the latter half of the 20th century: a fresh start.*

That day the social worker wasn't done. She turned a leaf of paper in Faith's file and began to read more notes.

"...one of your biological relatives is trying to reach you."

"Who?"

"We can't disclose that..."

"How long have they been trying to reach me?"

"They've sent several letters," the social worker said flatly.

Faith couldn't swallow. *I don't even know what I feel. My emotions are just out of reach and I can't put a name to them. Oh, my God, what's in those letters? The poor thing, she's been trying to reach me! I didn't know birth-mothers did that! I thought I was a burden, happily forgotten. I know it's her.*

The social worker promised to send Faith the typed-up pages she had been reading from. Something about a note in writing asking specifically who it was before they would let her know the author of the letters.

"You can scan it, if that's easier."

Faith's thoughts raced. She wrote the letter, mailed it, and after a surprisingly long wait got a phone call from the same social worker.

"Do we have permission to release your contact information to her?" *Her. Faith had sensed, without being told, it was her mother.*

"Y-yes. What's my birth-mother's name?"

"Ophelia. She lives overseas. That's why it took a while to contact her. We wanted to do it all in writing because we'd been threatened before with a lawsuit by an adoptive father after a birth-mother tried to contact a grown adoptee."

Faith had kept her parents informed about reaching out to the agency each step of the way. A thought passed through her mind: Maybe that adult who was adopted was still on good terms with what sounded like a domineering father. Or maybe that adult wasn't.

"Ophelia?" Faith wanted to make sure she was really hearing her mother's name.

"Yes, Ophelia, Faith," said the social worker, "Ophelia."

The prettiness of the name gave Faith shivers. Now she could also hear the warmth in the social worker's voice.

* * *

"I guess I'd given my consent to be contacted but up until then everything had taken so long and seemed so abstract that the actual phone call was a shock. I didn't know when it would happen, first of all," said Faith. "Second, my adoptive mother actually happened to be visiting and was reading to my girls.

"I get the call and my birth-mum has that midlantic accent of someone who's spent time back and forth on both sides of the Atlantic Ocean. She says she's leaving the next day to housesit in Spain, meeting her brother there, but wanted to first reach out to me beforehand.

"I hear the girls in the other room saying, 'Gam, please don't stop. Turn the page!' 'Gam' is what they call Mom and I guess she's listening too. Susan, my loyalties are going in a thousand directions and the guilt crowds out a lot of my memories."

Susan thought for a moment. "The nice thing about her writing you the letter, and then calling first, is you know you won't get rejected. What was it like getting that phone call?"

"For me, surprise and confusion.

"When I get off the phone. Mom and I talk and we agree there's no way Ophelia is going to Spain now. She'll change her mind and appear on my doorstep tomorrow morning. Isn't that what you'd do if you had a child out there? We both agree," said Faith.

"Oh, of course I would," said Susan.

"Except it doesn't happen. I'll tell you more about *that*. But what's really interesting is how it affected all of us." Faith reached for a two-person teapot in the center of the table and poured first Susan and then herself more *o-cha*. She brought the celadon-colored teacup to her lips and then paused, "Here's what I think: I sometimes think that I discovered as much about my adoptive family as I did about my birth-family from this search and reunion," Faith said.

"What are some of the takeaways?" asked Susan.

"Okay, I'd put it this way. The telephone call from my birth-mother re-opened the dark closet of adoption to let in a single ray of light that refracted with different hues off Mom, my children's father, my daughters and me. Mom told me once, afterward, that she had thought she was supportive of my following through and contacting my birth-mother. But driving home later, she felt like she'd been dropped in cement. It was the *first* time she'd ever really believed in such a thing as the subconscious," said Faith.

"I bet that statement is shorthand for a lot of things," said Susan.

"For sure; the overseas phone call reawakened memories of being diagnosed in her twenties with uterine cancer and having a hysterectomy to save her life. Mom told me that during her recovery the hospital had her room with a woman who had just had a baby!"

"Oh, God."

"My mother wondered if she hadn't squandered her artistic talent by raising kids. And, she shared this thought with me unapologetically. At the time I was proud to be her confidante even though it hurt. I have wondered if her infertility made her more ambitious: she was never satisfied with herself as-is, she had something to prove. She was jealous, I guess, that my birth-mother's artistic career was more of a going proposition than her own. It must have seemed to her like this birth-mother was going to have her cake and eat it, too: an artistic career, plus a daughter and grandkids," Faith explained.

"Pure fear," Susan said. "We were both from the time before open adoptions."

Faith nodded, "I know Mom was moved though when she received that handmade card from my birth-mother thanking her for raising me. Ophelia was wistful, she wrote that no reunion could equal the holidays, the little girl party dresses or the years together that my adoptive mother got to enjoy."

"What about...?"

"Him? My kids' dad had been mildly supportive of my looking up my adoption file: he wanted our kids to know the other half of their heritage. But he didn't like discussing any of the emotional aspects of this search and reunion," said Faith.

"You never told me that," said Susan.

Faith shrugged. She was trying to move past that marriage, "My eldest daughter was almost six, she wanted to know why her grandma couldn't have me in her tummy. My mother told her it got broken. Then she wanted to know why Ophelia had given me away. I told her that back then the rules were different and if you weren't married you weren't allowed to keep your baby. And then she got really upset and wanted to know if her grandparents couldn't be her grandparents anymore!"

"Oh, poor thing!"

"Right? I assured her that her grandparents were still her grandparents. A few times since then we've caught her threatening her younger sister with 'You're adopted,' or 'If you don't give that back I'm gonna put you up for adoption.' I was unnerved until some other mothers told me that's a normal taunt. It was new to me, not something you say if you've grown up in a family formed by adoption," Faith said.

"Yeah, no one ever said it to me. I wouldn't have used it on anyone either," said Susan, "You said Ophelia didn't visit right away..."

Faith nodded. "Ophelia still wasn't visiting but she did put me in touch with her elder sister, my aunt, Janice, who told me another story, about their mother. Their mother, my grandmother, took the Lexington Avenue bus one day and thought she saw a young woman who reminded her of Ophelia."

"When was this?" Susan asked.

"It was a few years ago, after Ophelia had begun contacting the adoption agency...

"So, as my biological grandmother watched this stranger, she felt more and more certain that the woman was the daughter Ophelia had given birth to years before. When my birth-grandmother got off the bus, instead of going home, she went to visit her daughter Janice up in Westchester County and for the first time told her about Ophelia's pregnancy and the missing granddaughter," Faith said.

Susan leaned forward, "Do you think...?"

"It is entirely possible that she saw me on that bus. I rode it regularly during that time and actually *only* during that time; I was arranging the television filming of a scene at Bloomingdale's Department Store on Lexington Avenue for a Christmas special.

"I've raked my memory trying to remember an old woman with hauntingly familiar features staring at me on a city bus. Sometimes I think I do remember someone staring at me with large brown eyes on the Lexington Avenue. I thought it was because the crew and I were speaking in Japanese. She had a pretty, round face under gray hair tied back in a bun, but I will never know for sure because my birth-grandmother died before I could meet her.

"If only the adoption agency had informed me immediately when my birth-mother tried to contact me! I could have met this grandmother! I could have told her I was okay and that my adoptive parents were good to me, and that I like the thought that she never forgot me," said Faith.

They were both silent for a few moments.

Then Faith continued, "With me pregnant at the time and now with the kids being young, I'm not leaving to visit Ophelia overseas. We do exchange airmail letters and speak by phone but she remains a cypher to me. She's cagey with information about my father or her own family tree, so learning about my own heritage turns into a game of cat and mouse, I'm not kidding. Worse, she talks about coming to visit, we even talk dates, usually around my birthday, and then she always has something come up. This just isn't what I expected," Faith said.

Susan listened with something to say, "For your sake, I wish she'd had therapy first. This isn't fair to you. Do you know the author Betty Jean Lifton?"

"Of course," said Faith, "everyone in the adoption world does. I've been reading everything I can get my hands on while I wait."

"I heard her speak once. She said that 'a birth-mother goes looking for her baby and instead she finds her trauma'. The baby is still gone, replaced by an adult. Instead, she's re-living feelings and memories from that pregnancy. How long did she put it off?"

"A visit? She hasn't visited and it's been three years since the phone call. Oh, you know, Mom said to me one day, 'It's a little like waiting for Godot.'"

Susan leaned forward, "The Samuel Beckett play?"

"Yeah, Mom was a Yalie and liked to quote stuff like that." Faith replied, "The conversation went something like this with Mom saying, 'These three years since Ophelia's phone call with no visit – especially the plans to visit on your birthday, the emotional energy they stirred up for everyone only to have her break them – are absurd; whatever our individual expectations of the reunion, we're still left waiting. Like Beckett's *Waiting for Godot*.'

"Then, I say, '*Waiting for Ophelia*. Mom, I thought you avoided absurdism? You even swore never to see a play by Edward Albee,' and I'm stunned when she says, 'Faith, I've thought about that since Ophelia's phone call. Since realizing there *is* a subconscious and I've got one too. For me, I now see, it wasn't that Albee wrote absurdist plays, it was that he wrote *adoption* plays.'"

"Sure," said Susan with excitement, "*Play about the Baby* or *Tiny Alice* or *The American Dream*."

"Right! And Mom agrees and says, 'adoption had more of an influence...no, *not* adoption, my *subconscious* had more of an influence on us than I realized. I'm sorry Ophelia doesn't come to visit. At first I was afraid she was going to steal you and my grandchildren –'

"Of course I tell Mom that no one could never do that. Then she asks me a terrific question: 'You've always been so adventurous, why wouldn't you search?! Was it because of me?' It's all happening fast. I don't think I answered her, maybe just shook my head, Susan, but the truth is it, searching, seemed too great a betrayal to even acknowledge enough to reject –"

"– too great a betrayal to even acknowledge enough to reject –"

"If that makes sense," added Faith.

"Yes, I get it," said Susan.

"I guess my subconscious had a role here too," Faith said.

"Then she shifts to 'We both thought she'd be on the next plane over from England, didn't we?'"

"That's how mothers think, isn't it?" said Susan.

Faith nods. "Then my mother says something like 'maybe there's two kinds of people in the world. Those who think about children and the next generation –' and I finish the thought, 'And those who don't. For whatever reason.' Then Mom nods, Susan, and we talked about the birds outside. Our family tradition was to keep binoculars by the birdfeeder window."

Faith fell silent, ruminating.

Susan let her, taking a few moments to look through email on her device, before looking up. "It seems a little like you'd rather talk about birds and binoculars right now too. That's okay." Then Susan scanned the *bento* box in front of her. "I don't want all this *wasabi*..."

Faith sounded relieved at the new topic, "I love *wasabi*! I'll take it."

Faith mostly lived her life and began skipping many of the ATC Monday nights. She did devour every search and reunion memoir she could get her hands on until she felt the kids were old enough or she couldn't stand to wait anymore and her adoptive parents offered to pitch in with the grandkids so she could fly to London and meet the elusive Ophelia, more than three years after they first spoke.

But first, she had some unfinished business before she boarded that jet.

>>> 2021, TOKYO & NEW YORK CITY

Faith knew that after decades of high-risk shoots and last-minute saves, her boss Ryuji Kato had reached a place as an executive producer in Japanese television where he was secure enough not to fear that every project was going to be his last. It helped that television was not yet a gig economy in Japan when he was coming up. He had created enough memorable stories for the morning news and entertainment circuit that his reputation was firmly fixed in the eyes of the studio. Faith was frustrated that the one place Ryuji deftly avoided traveling was New York City even though he was frequently on the road for assignments around the globe.

What it meant for Faith was that she had to lobby for face time with him in Japan. Once, when Tokyo was playing musical chairs with all the overseas bureaus and production houses, she booked her own flight and paid out of pocket to spend quality time with the rest of the show's staff to make the case for herself. That and leaning in at 3am post-air meetings probably saved her job. It helped that Faith spoke serviceable Japanese so no one felt like they were carrying her water for her.

Faith heard through the grapevine that Ryuji, while still keeping her at arm's length, approved of her. The feedback to him from the field crew was that she worked diligently, but that she also talked with her hands, laughed out loud and made a good drinking partner. Faith embodied what every schoolboy imagined when he heard the words *gaijin no onna no hito*, "a woman from a Western land". Her copper kettle colored hair had curls and her bright eyes glinted the gingery brown of ten-yen coins.

One rumor was that his ex-lover, a field producer named Fusako, and her mother were raising his son Noboru, here. Faith knew everyone here was tightlipped enough that he could have no idea that the Tokyo gossip had reached her.

He certainly might have wondered though when she proposed a documentary about the institution of adoption in America by phone, early afternoon his time.

Her story pitch to Ryuji this time was about the rights of people who were relinquished by a parent in America.

He interrupted before she really got started. "I find it amusing that you can just make an orphan a member of the family or make a foreigner a naturalized citizen. North America is very different from Japan, for sure," he said in a disapproving tone.

Then Ryuji seemed to convey his displeasure by rustling papers in the background as Faith launched in with "as they grow older, birth-fathers and male donors, men who didn't raise their children, are now testifying on behalf of those adoptees and donor-conceived people in state legislatures. They are redeeming themselves in the legislatures but also in a landmark test case that may go to the U.S. Supreme Court!... Ryuji-san, the sound quality isn't very good. Did you just put us on speaker?"

He grunted as he picked up the receiver. Faith wondered if this was about Noboru's existence.

"Do you know what 'adoption' is?" Faith used the English word, not knowing the Japanese for it.

Ryuji would never have been able to guess it had he not heard it once before on the lips of that American, Clay, years ago in Lima, Peru, that desert city by the sea. Ryuji grunted affirmatively that he had heard of the social services or agencies that matched *minashigo* or *koji*, parentless babies or children, with new families. He played along, but Faith could hear him fidgeting with what she remembered was a lime green stress ball at his desk.

Faith allowed a pause before she asked if he knew what a "birth-father" was and rushed on to explain it to him, saying, "A father who does not raise his child. A birth-father may or may not know he has a child. The child may or may not know who the birth-father is. 'Birth-father' is derived from the term 'birth-mother' which indicates a woman who gives birth to a child. It implies that someone else will mother that child, such as an adoptive mother. English speakers also use 'biological father', 'DNA father' or 'natural father'."

This could be getting far too close to Ryuji's own story

for comfort, and he might be wondering which of the Japanese cameramen in New York had set Faith up to call him – which wasn't the case at all. But how could she say that? On the other hand, if she said nothing would he pull the plug on this call right now?

She highlighted the potential US Constitutional issues. But more fun, Faith namechecked the classic rocker Tony Silvio of the Tony Silvio Project, mentioning interesting details about his reunion with his birth-daughter.

She was pleased when Ryuji actually hummed one of the Tony Silvio Project anthems, "Shoot the Alarm". She knew she had him now and told him the story of the Birth-Fathers' Club. She explained that the birth-fathers were supporting each other while waiting to testify in a case against big adoption and reproduction industries.

Ryuji cleared his throat and said summarily, *"Mou iin date,* from what you've given me all we have is a voice-over, we're not going to put budget on a reenactment. You need to get us backstage with the star witness, Tony Silvio, at a Tony Silvio Project concert. They're translating his rock memoir, *Birth of the True*, into Japanese. Get an advance copy. We'll also need courtroom access or the story will never get aired."

Faith was fairly sure she could get the credentials for the courtroom in the southern New York district but had no idea who to ask about anything in Japanese publishing. Or New York publishing off the top of her head. She'd get it but it would be a slog. Their connection crackled making Faith aware that Ryuji had paused a little over-long.

Then he said, "You have mentioned 'birth-father' twice. Is there some connection for you?"

She sucked in her breath. His hunch wasn't precise but it was right. "Actually," Faith began, "I was adopted. A *minashigo* or *koji*, an 'orphan', except my parents were alive. In adoption, most orphans aren't really orphans."

She paused to consider how he was hearing this, whether it was *iisugi*, an over-share, and decided to re-assure him. She also wanted Ryuji not to worry that the something in the air wasn't about his own past. She said, "I don't make it a secret. Fewer and fewer adoptees and adoptive parents do. It's mostly the donor-recipient families who are still building up secrets."

He gave Faith a provisional go-ahead pending a realistic shooting budget.

She let herself cry out with joy and then heard him chuckle. She knew though that he still had several touchpoints ahead where he could kill this story if he felt it was getting too close to him.

* * *

A few months later Ryuji committed a good chunk of the network budget to option a full season of something called "First World Baby" that included many segments to be shot in North America. His ex-lover Fusako would be senior producer and, Ryuji hoped, it would let Fusako learn on the job about child-friendly opportunities in New York. He called Fusako from an office phone behind closed doors to offer her the job himself.

He didn't raise the past but he used his gentlest voice, letting silences linger to give them more time on the connection.

Fusako sounded cool but accepted the project.

She had her pride, Ryuji understood that, so he made sure to also thank her before saying, "Talk to you again."

>>> 2021, NEW JERSEY

Faith and Susan had just placed their orders and were shaking their napkins into their laps. Faith explained, "I'm just realizing it's like that saying about if a tree falls in the woods and no one hears it. If you uncover something on a quest and have no one to share it with..."

"I knooooow. Come on, there's already enough suspense," Susan urged.

Faith raised her eyes mischievously, "I told you over the phone I had something to tell you—"

"Animal, vegetable, mineral?"

"Well," Faith began, "I told you how I searched the name that was on my original birth certificate, William Yard, which matched what Ophelia told me. I pulled up two-hundred of them east of the Mississippi online. I went by age and some tie to New York to narrow it down."

"And so...?"

"Last night, I sat down to make some phone calls—

three of them—to reach one of the men who could be my birth-father!"

"Awesome!"

"Oh, Susan, my hands shook. I was so nervous. Up until then I had been convincing myself that this search for my birth-father was just a "little" adventure. Then something clicked and I thought: of course, my hands should be shaking, I didn't know what I would find. Then I realized that this is probably 'normal' for finding your parent, even if 'finding' your parent isn't normal for most people," Faith said and then tossed her hair back and a few auburn brown rivulets caught the light as it cascaded across her shoulder.

Susan added thoughtfully, "I can't even imagine what it's like to grow up in a family you *are* related to. I can't imagine what it's like never to have to search in order to meet all your blood relatives, you know?"

Faith smiled, "I never put it that way, but yes. I almost think it's weird to grow up *knowing* your biological parents and *knowing* your brothers and sisters. Other people must take it for granted."

"But back to you," Susan said.

Faith continued, "None of the three names matched up exactly with what I knew about my birth-father."

"I'm so sorry," said Susan.

"Well, I'm grateful to Barbara and Pam pointing me to Bert Hirsch who drafted the Indian Child Welfare Act," Faith said. "Now that I'm doing the research for the documentary, it's really sinking in what he did. He and two congressional aids drafted and passed the ICWA years

ahead of the United Nations Hague Conventions supporting ethical adoptions, and fighting human trafficking, or
establishing the rights of children."

Susan leaned forward, "If the UN wasn't even doing
anything, where'd this law come from? I think this was the
tail end of the post-war Baby Scoop era when most agencies and states or provinces operated comfortably under a
cloak of darkness and just came in to scoop up babies."

"Well, apparently, he said they never set out to make
a law. If I got it right, they called him in for a single
case where a Native American child was removed from
the grandmother's loving care. The only reason given was
that the parents weren't present. Social workers came in
and placed the child with waiting White people. Fighting
that removal was the scope of the original case. But then
they did a survey of the reservation and found this happening to one in four children!"

"How did no one know?" Susan asked.

"They were whisked away from the reservation, and
because families were rural, and ashamed, they thought it
was their personal tragedy," Faith said.

"A case of the personal *is* political, huh?" said Susan,
"They didn't know it was happening across the reservation because people didn't see it or talk about it."

"Right. Bert and other staffers figured it couldn't be
just this one tribe. To confirm that, though, they worked
with tribal governments to conduct surveys across reservations around the country and the numbers are worse
than what we already knew for the Baby Scoop era,"
Faith said.

"That was several million babies," Susan remembered aloud.

"Across a much larger population. For Indigenous Americans the range was twenty-five to thirty-five percent of the kids, with no priority placed on keeping them with family like that grandmother," Faith sniffed and massaged her temples. Then she tried rubbing her eyes as though it would make the sorrow go away before she continued, "It wasn't about determination of safety, that's not what ICWA is about. It's about what culture or family an Indigenous child is raised in once it's determined parents –"

"Ohh, that's so sad. That's one child out of every three or four! It's a tragedy. Personally, my adoptive mother was great and I think some adoptions have to happen, but THIS. It's like Custer's ghost came back to steal a third of all Indian children and erase a third of the future of the tribe and the culture. My mother wouldn't have wanted a child under those conditions," said Susan.

"And now, back to Bert," Faith said.

Susan added, "And *your* search after finding out you're Indigenous. Did they name a tribe in your non-identifying information?"

"No," Faith answered, "Once I got proactive, those two women from the ATC meeting, Barbara and Pam, pointed me to Bert who pointed me to an Iroquois historian upstate. It was a long shot. I mentioned her, right? She was hopeful at first, saying there had been some members with the last name Yard. In the end, though, she couldn't pin anything down."

"At one of the meetings you and Rita looked up something with Mormons too," said Susan.

"That was Rita. She reached out to them. She's one of the first search angels I met. They went through the database of social security death benefits, thought they had the right Bill Yard. When Rita and I got the copy of the certificate back, he's described as 'Negro'. Look at me. You wouldn't even guess Indigenous unless I told you," said Faith.

"So, none of the three Bills you called turned out either?"

Faith sighed and shook her head.

Susan looked at Faith with an I-have-an-idea expression. "You already know the detective Fred Kouyoumjian from the Adoption Triad Circle. Hire him! I hate seeing you this way."

Faith nodded and looked down, stirring milk into her tea. Their checks arrived and they sat a little longer in comfortable silence.

"Susan, I don't know. Usually I'd want to give him a shot but I just have a feeling it won't work. Or I'm not ready for it to work..." Out of nowhere it got harder for Faith to swallow. She felt that rogue wave pushing her with an emotional force that knocked the wind out of her. She wanted to cry and instead silently ached.

"Faith?" Susan must have seen it.

Faith was afraid that if she tilted her chin up now Susan would see too much in her eyes. Instead, she kept her lashes down and didn't answer. She forced an apologetic laugh.

Susan spoke anyway. "Hey, Faith. Did you ever hear that song, 'Come on, come on'?"

Faith felt the tension lift from her shoulders and the muscles around her eyes relax. Suddenly she wasn't straining to keep them clear. She sighed, put on a smile and shook her hair back. She was able to look Susan square in the eyes now.

Ah, Susan, wherever this conversation leads us will be better than where I just was. Faith answered Susan, "No, I don't think so. But maybe if you hum it..."

Softly, so the other tables wouldn't hear, Susan began: *Come on come on, it's getting late now / Come on come on, take my hand*

Faith recognized the song as Susan continued, "...*It's a need you never get used to, so fierce and so confused / It's a loss you never get over the first time you lose....*"

Faith masked her sob as a cough and grabbed her tumbler just in time to silence it with ice water. She felt Susan reach out and *take my hand.*

Then Susan was saying something to keep the table conversation going, "...Mary Chapin Carpenter. I don't think it's about adoptees or adoptive parents or birth-parents. But there's something..."

Faith returned Susan's finger squeeze and decided she would get Fred's number from the ATC roster tonight and hire him immediately.

Susan was saying, "It's a pop song so it's gotta be a faded romance, but even so... I think Maya Angelou once said, 'We're more alike than unalike,' and yeah, for some of us, it comes earlier than others: *the first time you lose.*"

>>> 2021, NEW YORK CITY

FF Documentary notes from FG:

Pre-production: Research and writing, interview and location scouting, scheduling shoot days. This will take approximately 4-6+ weeks.

Production: Depends on Covid variants, additional travel restrictions, and courthouse closings. Approximately 1-2 weeks.

Post-production: Editorial, animation, motion graphics, audio design, mastering, and delivery. Approximately 2-6+ weeks.

Ryuji Kato got the budget that brought Faith a full documentary crew for taping in the Park Avenue suite of Ted Landtsman. A wiry attorney just this side of grizzled, he still wielded the power of his winsome grin. About a dozen men, dressed down, sat on leather sofas lining the suite's wainscoting or pulled up to the long mahogany conference table in state-of-the-art ergonomic chairs. They were trial witnesses, recruited by Ted's staff through carefully worded advertisements for birth-fathers and donors. The men who agreed to be witnesses were getting together outside of prep for the case and calling themselves 'The Birth-Fathers' Club'.

They all had vaxx cards as they would be no good to Ted if the courthouse barred their entrance. As it was, the trial schedule was up in the air because the justice complex was shut down for in-person hearings and Faith knew this might be their last taping for a while on this documentary.

This would be a landmark case and Faith took it seriously but right now she had to make sure they captured the visual details. They might seem small but they added to the richness of the storytelling. With that in mind, Faith tapped Sumi-san, the cameraman, and pointed to Tony Silvio of the Tony Silvio Project. The lanky rocker was in black fringes that purpled at the ends like his shoulder-length hair. It worked well on him. Sumi-san captured it perfectly, starting at Tony Silvio's handmade leather boots, capturing the long femurs, and then his floral sleeves that ended with one arm supporting his ringed-fingers and dimpled chin while the other draped across a bust of Themis, goddess of Justice and the Law. Tony was listening attentively to Ted. Sumi-san demonstrated his sixth sense by swinging the lens in Ted's direction just as the attorney excused himself from Tony Silvio and strode to the front of the room.

Ted sat on his desk and turned a chair around backwards to raise his feet. Sumi-san caught this detail with his camera. A short man using the height of the desk to become more imposing. The chair also kept Ted's feet from dangling. Sumi-san crouched down to catch Ted from a flattering angle before he began speaking.

"Let me explain something. Even though we were able to get the law passed in the legislature, the adoption industry is suing to get the law quashed. They want an injunction until a judge decides if the law is legal, in this case, whether it violates some guy's right to privacy if his kid finds him.

"They found an anonymous sperm donor and a birth-father to be fronts, to be the plaintiffs, but the industry is footing the bill. They've given us a test case. The legislative success they're resisting already shows our cause is *popular*; now we have to show it's *right*."

Faith motioned for Sumi-san to keep rolling.

"A quick history," Ted continued, "Just a few years ago the adoption and donor industries tried to claim they were 'protecting' the privacy of birth-mothers and egg donors."

Back in the editing room they'd intersplice this from Ted with Susan's answer to the interview question a few days ago about the low point of her reunion. Susan had said, "When my birth-mother said she couldn't identify my birth-father. Also learning that the adoption and donor industries, especially the gray market donor banks, are once more trying to take away our birthrights under the guise of 'protecting' someone. First it was birth-mothers. Then, because birth-mothers themselves overwhelmingly spoke out in enough places that the industries switched to a new tactic: 'protecting' birth-fathers and 'no contact' donors, even after all the fraud that's come to light! Maybe *because* of it?"

Ted was still holding the attention of the men standing or sitting around his office. "...It was around the time one state voted in a referendum to restore heritage equality to adoptees, but the industries decided to set up a test case to challenge it. Heritage equality means equal access to your original birth certificate and other relevant files for everyone, regardless of the details of their origins.

"As many of you already know, they recruited six birth-mothers to be plaintiffs in a test case to roll back heritage equality. They didn't expect that over eight-hundred birth-mothers and female donors would sign a petition in support of equality for adoptees and donor-conceived people – that's DCPs – as we say. The petition explained that they did not want to impose secrets on the adults they gave life to. Giant rout for the industries," Ted said.

"Okay, reaction shots," Faith whispered to Sumi-san. Sumi-san began a slow pan of the men as they listened to Ted.

"This time, the industries are back and claiming to speak for birth-*fathers*. Two reasons. Because birth-fathers don't show up to testify, by and large. And historically because birth-fathers have been the parent that didn't sign adoption relinquishment papers.

"New York's legislature overturned its secrecy laws first with a compromise bill. Then a group out of Brooklyn mounted a statewide petition that upped it to full equality, no provisions, no compromises. But the industry is mounting a rearguard action – not a true legal term – by continuing to defend heritage *in*equality. This time the plaintiffs are a 'no contact' anonymous male donor and a birth-father, JohnDoe1 and JohnDoe2. I'll be damned if I'll let them win!"

Faith checked the timestamp. This is where they'd insert clips from a donor-conceived teen with a large following on TikTok and other social media who had already nicknamed the plaintiffs BabyDaddyJoe and DeadbeatDoe.

Faith hesitated to insert her voice but she wanted Ted's answer on tape, so she asked the question and stayed behind the cameraman so they'd get Ted looking straight in the lens.

Ted started to search for her but quickly shifted to the lens, "If they win at the superior court level, we appeal the ruling all the way up to the U.S. Supreme Court. If *we* win the test case, the industries have invested so much that they won't back down gracefully and will appeal too. The appeal will wind its way up all the levels of state Appeals. We – or our adversaries – then have an automatic right to file a cert to the U.S. Supreme Court from the Second Circuit where New York is because there are several federal issues involved.

"Put in plain English, we will fight on appeal all the way up to the U.S. Supreme Court if necessary! We've got ourselves a test case here. And let's be honest, guys, if you never did anything for your biological children before, *now you get to do right by them.*"

Ted animatedly launched into the details, moving from bookcase to mahogany conference table to an inlaid sideboard with a cut crystal decanter set from which he poured Tony Silvio a whiskey.

When the rocker waved it away, Ted remembered that Tony was in recovery and gamely poured him a tall tumbler of club soda, downing the single malt himself.

Ted continued, "The two best ways to prevent the creation or maintenance of a separate class of people who are denied heritage rights based on origin, is twofold..."

Faith noticed that the crew was still dwelling on ambiance shots: the sun coming through window slats, someone's polished shoes, this was too much. Faith understood it meant the crew's comprehension or attention was wandering.

"*Achi!*" she whispered in Japanese, "Get back to the lawyer."

Sumi-san swiveled just in time to get Ted pounding a fist into his palm.

"You gentlemen are here to help kill the privacy argument once and for all.

"But we are bringing this argument together with a second argument, invoking the Equal Protection clause of the U.S. Constitution. We call this taking 'one bite of the apple'."

Faith had googled this last night for the documentary, "The 14th Amendment, right?" This was the stuff people went to jail for, even died for throughout history. Faith got a lump in her throat. To her, when a non-adoptee asked, "Why do you need heritage equality?" it was a little like asking "Why should you have freedom of speech like everyone else?" Maybe that's why she, like Betty Jean Lifton, liked to describe this as a hero's journey.

Ted agreed, "Yes, thank you, this is the 14th Amendment of the Constitution. And the strict scrutiny standard applies to discrimination against adoptees and DCPs that the industries have promulgated through state legislatures, just like it applies to discrimination based on race, gender, and sexual orientation."

"What is the strict scrutiny standard?" It was a birth-father's voice Faith recognized well, Clay Dennen, who was not only selected by Ted Landtsman's team to testify but was also designated as the media contact for the Birth-Fathers' Club.

"The standard holds that there must be 'compelling governmental interest' served by amending, redacting, or creating legal fictions in the birth certificates of DCPs and adoptees by not providing their biological parents' names. This legal fiction continues to harm individuals and their right to know their history. In addition, when adoption or donor contracts, to which adoptees and DCPs aren't even a party, strip them and their descendants in perpetuity of heritage rights enjoyed by all others, we have created a second class of citizens."

As Ted turned toward representatives of the Adoption Triad Circle, who Faith knew were all involved in leg-islative activities in the tri-state area, she directed the cameraman to pan over to them.

He said pointedly, "This doesn't take away from the importance on the ground of state-by-state battles waged through the legislature. But these court cases are your potential air cover."

Ted continued, "Once we start appearing on news sites and broadcasts, once we start testifying at the State House, we make it easier for other DNA fathers to come out. It makes it easier for the larger society to understand that helping adoptees who are searching is a worthy cause, that 'test-tube babies' or 'adopted children' grow up and have the same rights to their heritage as everyone else. A victory at the highest level might speed reform, set a precedent that can lift almost a century of imposed shame."

Clay started clapping and the rest of the room joined in. Faith tried to keep her emotions out of it as she prepared to approach some of the witnesses to set up individual interviews but inside, she was brimming with pride at what they were doing, joy at the chance at a Supreme Court case, and anger at what had been stolen from her and from other adoptees and DCPs.

>>> 2022, New Jersey

Faith found that the past few months had lifted her to a different emotional shoreline than the last time she'd met Susan for lunch. Then she'd just struck out with three phone calls to leads who turned out not to be her father. Now she stood in the kitchen, excited after pressing Susan's number. She'd waited until after the kids went to bed. When Susan answered, Faith barely said hello before jumping to, "Susan, we found him! Bill! Fred Kouyoumjian, the PI from the group? I did hire him. Then he traced Bill's phone number. It's him, it's my birth-father!"

"Oh, my gosh, congratulations. You're sounding so much better. Have you called him yet?"

"No. I will. Just checkin' in first."

"I'm here for ya. How are you feeling?"

"In charge. And not in charge. I kicked off this search for my birth-father in a way I didn't with the reunion with my birth-mother: the search is mine but the reunion is out of my hands," said Faith.

"I agree," said Susan. "The searches can empower us but the reunions or rejections may be out of our hands. I'm gonna steal that line: 'the search is mine but the reunion is out of my hands'." Susan laughed before turning serious, "I don't think the average person gets that this isn't just like their grandparents doing an embroidered family tree. It's not a pastime, it has the power of a quest. Maybe only other adoptees and donor-conceived people take *this* quest."

Part 2

FAITH
"The low points of my reunion? They came right on the heels of the honeymoons. What do I mean? Well, I realized that even though Ophelia's phone call had ripped off *my* scab of spiritual denial, *she* wouldn't be visiting any time soon. On the other hand, searching for my birth-father was a journey of empowerment: discovering the search and reunion community; making heart connections with adoptees and donor-conceived people; and, intellectual engagement with the rock star of the adoption world, Betty Jean Lifton. These steeled me for another dark night of the soul...."

SOLOMON
"The low points of my reunion? Let me just say first of all that I don't regret it for a minute. But Susan looking me straight in the eye as she described what it was like for her birth-mother Noklek. You know, later that week with a scotch, I just let myself imagine what it must have been

like for Noklek, a country girl alone and pregnant, and then leaving her, our, newborn baby. Those two moments were the low points."

SUSAN
"When my birth-mother said she couldn't identify my birth-father. Also learning that the adoption and donor industries, especially the gray market donor banks, are once more trying to take away our birthrights under the guise of 'protecting' someone. First it was birth-mothers. Then, because birth-mothers themselves overwhelmingly spoke out in enough places that the industries switched to a new tactic: 'protecting' birth-fathers and 'no contact' donors, even after all the fraud that's come to light! Maybe *because* of it?"

~ 3 ~

BILL 2022, NEW YORK CITY

The call.

I heard a woman's voice, trembling slightly say, "Is this Bill Yard? I hope you're sitting down. We've never met, but I was born on March 22nd, 1972."

I almost laugh when I realize who the call is from. If you don't laugh you gotta cry, I tell myself. I shake my head, maybe to clear it.

I tell her, "I think I know who you are but just hold on a minute. I want to switch phones."

I go into my study and close the door before picking up the receiver. Then I sit behind my desk and lean back so I can see the shelf of rock and roll memoirs on the left wall.

"Hello," I begin and then blurt out, "I knew some day I'd get this call." Can you feel dread and relief at the same time, I wonder?

She tells me the town she lives in. I haven't heard of it. There is almost nothing I do know about her, my daughter! I ask, "What's your name?"

"Faith."

I say nothing and Faith rushes in, "Faith Givvers, no pun intended."

I bet I know people Faith would like to hear about, given her connection to Japan and adoption. I tell Faith about the set of parents whose children I met when I taught private school, Betty Jean Lifton who wrote a memoir about being adopted, and her husband Robert J. Lifton, founder of Doctors Against Nuclear Proliferation who treated atomic bomb survivors in Japan.

I read Betty Jean Lifton's adoption memoir, attended one of the husband's lectures. In fact, I checked out each of her books on adoption from the library and read them during my lunch break rather than having them at home. I never approached her to discuss them. Faith's response surprises me.

"I know her," said Faith, "well, I know of her."

Ophelia. I feel uncomfortable. What I did to Ophelia. What I did to our child. I also feel relief to hear from a safe, grown Faith – after carrying this secret for decades – she's okay and yet my guilt curdles any fatherly affection I *should* have for Faith. Curdles my affection but not my curiosity for Faith and some kind of attachment I already feel.

She lives in a suburb near the city. We make plans to meet midweek which turns out to be Ash Wednesday.

She asks me, "How will I recognize you?"

Of course. My daughter but she has never seen me. I find myself answering, "I'll wear a carnation."

"Sounds like a movie."

"Yeah, that's probably where I got it from. Speaking of which –"

"Yes?"

"We were going to name you Claudia."

"You had a name picked out?"

"Yes. I'll tell you who Claudia is when I see you."

We hang up.

I stay in my chair, lean forward a little to run my fingers along its edge and then toss a gaze over at the bookcase.

All my witnesses.

The newest one is a rock memoir you can't escape called *Birth of the True* by the Tony Silvio Project frontman. Tony Silvio's daughter found him through a DNA test. That much I – and everyone who isn't hiding in a cave – knew. I bought *Birth of the True* and it doesn't matter to me that the memoir title comes not from a Tony Silvio Project original but from a cover the group did of the song by Aztec Camera.

Birth of the True is just one of about a dozen rock memoirs on my bookshelf that might look like just the collection of an aging fan. But it isn't the music and the high times that attract me. Buried within this genre are the stories of other men who either got a surprise or shared this secret I've been carrying for decades: fatherhood.

Hank Williams, Sr., whose daughter published a book on proving his paternity. Famously, there is Mick Jagger, Keith Richards, and Brian Jones of the early Rolling Stones – or rather the birth-mother whose memoir *Not Fade Away* tells of relinquishing their baby – as well as Rod Stewart, Roger Daltrey, Steven Tyler and Tom Petty.

David Crosby was briefly an anonymous sperm donor before becoming an involved parent. I don't have a memoir by him, but I pull up and tap "I'll Cast a Spell on You" by the musician trained in opera, who managed to be a pioneer of shock rock while simultaneously delivering R & B and soul: Screamin' Jay Hawkins. Over thirty-seven adults claimed Screamin' Jay Hawkins as their birth-father while he actually claimed that he fathered over fifty kids on the road.

* * *

Ophelia and I met while we were separately painting in acrylics at the Cloisters. It was the beginning of summer and I had set up my easel on one of the riverbanks below the monastery-like buildings. I felt a little like a figure in a Bruegel painting myself, set up below the medieval edifice of the Cloisters that had been transported brick by brick from Europe and reassembled on a bluff between the Hudson and East Rivers.

In the morning, I didn't see her yet because I faced my canvas toward the East River. At noon I folded up my gear – tubes of paint, brushes, canvases, folding easel – and carried them under my arm to the opposite slope overlooking the Hudson River. That's where I saw her, already absorbed in sketching on her small canvas the outlines of a fresh landscape.

She was striking, in a full-length sundress, scarlets and purples, her art satchel open and her colors scattered on a drop-cloth of paint-splattered batik.

We were keenly aware of one another even before I walked over. I watched her in silence, then offered her half my tuna sandwich. She barely looked at me as she shook her head but it was then that I noticed her dimples, her cheekbones, her hips on a low folding tripod seat. I went back to my own easel a few yards away, keenly aware of her nearness.

As the shadows grew longer that afternoon, I wet my throat with water from an old Swiss army flask, carefully replacing the metal cup. I put the felt encased canteen back between the leather straps of my satchel before walking over to her.

I watched her strokes quietly for a few minutes and then commented on the sunlight coming in low over the Hudson to our west. She turned, a graceful opening of her shoulders, her collarbone and chest now directly below me. She was charming. That is a word you use about Ophelia, charming, delightful, with, I would come to discover over the coming weeks, a cleverness, a quickness of mind matched by her deftness of hand. She was artful.

Our time together was impulsive in many ways. She appeared at my drafting table at CBS Records or I at hers in Hallmark's old studios. We broke out together as soon as the wall clock clicked five o'clock. We painted together, once even on a Saturday night at a piano bar in the

Village. Our attraction was intuitive, we painted, went on picnics, attended outdoor concerts and arthouse films. I never brought her to my parents' or my grandparents' in our urban Indian enclave although they knew about her. Much of her family was in England although she had a newly married sister in Canada, a brother stationed at a listening post in Misawa, Japan, and her mother in Forest Hills, a Queens neighborhood.

The real reason I didn't show her around was that I was already engaged to be married. The weight of all my decisions that summer and autumn has grown heavier with understanding. I was engaged already to Rémy.

Rémy was dedicated to our relationship, even-keeled, and away on sabbatical. I told Ophelia one night that I had a girlfriend, not a fiancé, who was away. Ophelia drew away from me like a kitten who has been struck. I knew this wasn't fair, not just because Ophelia was trusting, but because I chose to tell her this in a darkened theater, among other couples outlined in silver light. In a moment I reached for her and in a few more moments she nuzzled back into my arms.

I remember the movie, "8½" by Federico Fellini, starring Claudia Cardinale and Marcello Mastroianni at an arthouse theater in the Village. Another night we saw "The Leopard" or *Il Gattopardo* by Luchino Visconti, starring Burt Lancaster, Alain Delon, Paolo Stoppa, and again Claudia Cardinale.

One afternoon I read in *Variety* or some other rag

that Claudia filmed both at the same time, moving between them. I imagined myself not as Mastroianni or Burt Lancaster, but the mysterious Claudia, moving between sets, between directors. There were many times I placed the phone in the receiver after speaking either to Rémy or Ophelia, only to pick it up again, listen for a new dial tone, and call my other lover. Rémy was the Visconti, subdued, reasonable, and focused. Ophelia was Fellini's stylish improvisation, creative chaos, and a slight sadness that made her infinitely sympathetic to my lost soul. She told me, more than once, that she had just lost her father, her brother and sister were gone, and she was living with her newly widowed mother in an outer borough.

Our lost souls recognized each other.

Nevertheless, a few months later I made the decision that I didn't believe in soul mates and I chose Rémy. I made the decision to abandon my pregnant lover and our child, Faith, for the one to whom I was already betrothed. Ophelia and I had even picked out the name Claudia if the baby were a girl.

A few years later I made the decision to abandon working in the arts with its studio camaraderie to enter teaching. That's how I met Betty Jean and Robert J. Lifton – through their children – before I moved to a more lucrative position in the City bureaucracy.

When Rémy, back from sabbatical, suggested we go see the "Pink Panther" starring Claudia Cardinale and David Niven at a '60s film week, I was struck dumb. I suppose we talked about Claudia's other films but I said nothing of the earlier decision with Ophelia to refer to our child as Claudia.

Not that night but soon though, I promised myself I would tell Rémy about the pregnancy and my complete and utter confusion about what to do.

I suppose I will tell Faith when I meet her about Rémy's and my decisions that didn't unfold.

Those decisions made my life more stable but left me an angry man. I don't even know myself why I was so angry, but I noticed that what others accept with good grace leaves me reacting. I am angry at all the decisions like these that I was forced to make. What others shake off, I nurse as just one more unintended consequence.

~ 4 ~

FAITH 2022, NEW YORK CITY & NEW JERSEY

FF Documentary notes from RK: Faith! *Guzen*/Coincidences never work in storytelling! Cut Robert J. Lifton – a Japanese audience will never believe the coincidence/*guzen* that your birth-father knew the doctor who treated Hiroshima atomic bomb survivors in Japan. Cut Betty Jean Lifton too. Again, *guzen* never work in storytelling.

FF Documentary notes from FG: Ryuji-san, your guidance that coincidences don't work in fiction is most helpful. Fortunately, this is not fiction and *moshikashite*, these two true synchronicities will resonate especially with two audiences: *Yappari*, for Japanese, Robert J. Lifton-*sensei wa hibakusha no keiken ya Hiroshima no jotai wo tsutaeta o-isha-san nan' desu.* For the adoption and donor-conception constellation, Betty Jean Lifton popularized early research on the impact of relinquishment and attachment *desukara*.

At this Monday night ATC meeting, when one of the facilitators called the number for Faith's turn, Faith shared that she had *finally located her birth-father*.

If Motown invented the wall of sound, these search and reunion circles must have invented the wall of love. It sounded like all forty people in the room called out "congratulations." The room hummed, almost in unison.

"So you found him, after all!"

"What did you say to him?"

"Have you met yet?"

Faith answered, "We're having lunch next Wednesday."

"You just made my day!"

"This is great news."

"Enjoy this time."

Faith reached for some crudité that was on a big plastic Costco platter in the middle of the table, and noticed that a few other people were reaching for snacks.

"Aren't you glad you didn't give up? Three years it's been."

"You've waited so long for this. It's good to see your patience pay off."

"It just goes to show there's always hope."

"Hope."

"There's always hope."

"I'm so happy for you but I am also jealous!

The adopted men and birth-fathers were the most enthusiastic. One asked her, "How the hell did you pull that off?"

She answered, with some pride, "Okay, here's how to crack the system. Phase one was three years ago. I went to the library to use some software that contained two national telephone directories...."

As she continued speaking, Faith spied a bowl of chips coming her way. This was one of the heartwarming and sometimes disconcerting things about the circle. No matter how serious the emotional discussions, you'd never go hungry here.

She demurred but passed the bowl on to the next person. The pause let someone named Jeremy break in with a wink, "Finding no obituaries was a good thing: either your birth-father is alive or maybe immortality runs in your gene pool!"

She wasn't sure she got the joke but laughed anyway, and then it occurred to her to share something that might help others: "Every state is different, but the birth archives in the public library date from when adoptees could access their original birth certificate using the later one that the state issued with their adoptive parents' names on it. Both the amended adoptive birth certificate and the original birth certificate are stamped with the same number. Even with the industry trying to have them removed away from public access, they say on social that the Mormons or AncestrologyDNA may move it online so we can get around the industry."

"Praise the Church of Latter-Day Saints."

"Amen."

"Amen."

Then Faith carefully explained to the group about Fred's having a sympathetic cop run a DMV check. From that he was able to get Bill's phone number.

Fred was sitting right there; he usually made every first Saturday of the month meeting. She'd heard others' stories, often including Fred as the hired detective breaking their case. Now she was the one telling her story.

Someone raised a hand tentatively, then asked, "I wonder if that's legal?" It was Todd, one of the birth-fathers. He rocked back in his chair. "The records that are legal to view are the public record documents like amended birth certificates. It's not lost on me that the DMV check that helped you, Faith, is a violation of laws designed to protect FBI informants. I'm not criticizing your methods, I'm just sayin'."

A few scattered pairs were speaking in sidebars Faith couldn't hear that made her nervous. Before she could think of a response, Susan spoke up for her, "I think of it as being like a conscientious objector. These are laws that only apply to us and our children—like Jim Crow laws only applied to Black Americans in the South, or indecency laws were meant to persecute homosexuals—these laws create a separate class of citizen that it's okay to discriminate against. These laws shut out adoptees and all of our descendants. Donor-conceived people and their descendants, too. We are denied birthright information about our heritage because unjust laws are on the books."

The room had changed, silent now as people considered what she said.

Susan went on. "Thoreau taught civil disobedience to laws upholding slavery. The Underground Railroad was started to flout the Fugitive Slave Law and the Dred Scott decision that tried to force White people in free states to send people who had escaped the institution of slavery back to their former owners. When a law is wrong morally, Thoreau argued, civil disobedience to that law is the only moral response."

Another parent, a birth-mother, chimed in to Todd, "They're treating you birth-fathers like you're in a witness protection program, too, like birth-mothers. From our own children. What kind of people do they think we are?"

That question lingered uncomfortably in the suddenly silent room.

* * *

Faith decided to tell them about the shared connection with Betty Jean Lifton. They all knew her as BJ because she was the rock star of the adoption constellation and many people sitting in the room had read her memoir and other non-fiction books as Bill had. Someone gave Faith BJ's number.

Faith had no idea what she'd do if BJ didn't remember

Bill. She waited until the day after the ATC meeting to call her.

"Bill! Bill! Bill! Oh, I remember him, he was a wonderful teacher. How do you know him?"

"He's my birth-father. We've just reconnected..."

"That's wonderful! My son and daughter had him in middle school."

"Yes, and he told me he read your memoir, too. And that he went to a lecture about Physicians for Nuclear Responsibility that your husband gave."

"Have you met face to face yet?"

"No, that's tomorrow. We've spoken once on the phone. That's when he told me about you," Faith said.

"Let me know how it goes..."

That tapped out the details BJ remembered about Bill so they ran through their list of mutual acquaintances. Then Faith turned the conversation to a line in one of BJ's books: "We do not know if Moses ever asked, 'Who am I?' We do know what happened when Oedipus asked the question." Faith had always been haunted by the contrast between BJ's careful research into Greek and Roman myth and her lack of any into the myth BJ grew up celebrating every spring with her Jewish adoptive parents: the story of Moses the adoptee!

Why the willful ignorance? As for her Greek hero, Oedipus, did she really know his story, or just one version of it? BJ knew the play "Oedipus Rex" by Sophocles, she described it in her books. In that telling, Oedipus murders his father, sleeps with his

mother, and when he realizes what he's done, puts out his own
eyes. Freud coined the term Oedipal complex for incest.

But did she know the original Greek myth? Oedipus is not
deceived about his origins, therefore tragedy is averted, and he
enjoys a long reign. His clear vision enables him to save a city
by solving the riddle of the Sphinx. Oedipus, and other adoptee
heroes like Moses, Gilgamesh, Hiawatha, or Romulus and Remus,
received the gift of awareness.

Faith wasn't sure how to begin but said into the receiver, "It was Oedipus' inquisitiveness as a searcher, his
awareness, that enabled him to save a city from destruc-
tion by solving the riddle of the Sphinx – just as he solved
the riddle of his origin, BJ. You may remember that riddle:
What walks on four legs in infancy, two legs in its prime,
and three legs in old age? The answer is humanity. Humans crawl on four legs in infancy, walk upright in their
prime, and use a third leg, a cane, in old age..."

"Ah," said BJ, "so of course search and reunion brings
him back into humanity, into belonging and integration."

"Yes, and at the same time being adopted (like growing
up between two faiths, two races, or two countries) gives
you a different take on life; maybe Oedipus' different
perspective allowed him to see answers that others could
not. Just like Moses is able to 'see' the Burning Bush or
the Ten Commandments for founding a civilized society,"
Faith said.

BJ said, "I just don't like organized religion. Does *any-*
one go to church or synagogue anymore? So, remind me
of the plot again."

The "plot"? I get that we are not reminiscing about childhood Passovers. She prefers that our childhood memories be distilled as plot or mythology. No judgement.

Faith sketched the story: Joseph being sold into slavery by his jealous brothers but rising in Pharaoh's court to be a trusted advisor. Joseph forgiving his brothers in a time of famine when they arrive as beggars, ultimately leading the Hebrew tribes to settle in Egypt. A new Pharaoh, after generations, enslaves the Hebrews and decrees he will kill all their male babies. One baby boy, cast in a basket onto the Nile, is rescued by Pharaoh's daughter who raises him as a prince of Egypt.

Moses, as an adult, sees an Egyptian slavedriver beat a Hebrew slave and lashes out, killing the Egyptian. He flees to the country of Midian, where he works close to the land as a shepherd, until the day God sends him on a search by appearing to him in a burning bush and revealing the names of his birth-father and forefathers.

"Ah, Faith, you see! Moses was also an Angry Young Man. He kills just as Oedipus did," BJ said.

"But that doesn't speak for most of us adoptees. His concern for identity, for what makes community and belonging..." and Faith rattled off all of Moses' Bible-worthy achievements, especially his establishing a system of judgeships, his understanding the labor it takes to form something greater than ourselves.

Faith and BJ moved on to the exodus from Egypt itself when God visits ten plagues on the land to convince Pharaoh to let his people go. Faith recited them. For an adoption project Faith worked on with Susan, they interpreted each plague as the challenges faced by all three sides of the triangle: adoptee/donor-conceived person, adoptive parents/recipient parents, and DNA parents.

Faith said, "The last plague, the death of the firstborn –"

"I've always hated the *seder* for this. This bloodthirstiness –"

"The play *Oedipus Rex* is fairly gory too, isn't it? And we always pour out some of our wine to grieve the Egyptian losses at each of the plagues, they are God's children too –"

"Joseph Campbell called all of Exodus just a collection of Middle Eastern myths," BJ said.

Faith felt like she'd been slapped. Not by BJ but by Joseph Campbell. Faith answered her slowly, "It sounds like Campbell may have been a product of his time and privilege, but I can treat Hebrew culture with the *same* respect he treated Greek and Roman culture." Faith was roiled inside, not sure what she felt toward BJ, a writer of beautiful non-fiction prose. *Was BJ was one of those self-hating Jews, by adoption or birth, who needed to learn anti-anti-Semitism?*

Faith began again, "Maybe this interpretation of the last plague is more helpful. It's the death of a dream for a biological connection between parent and child, the death of that dream that led hopefully to acceptance before adoption or donor-conception."

They remained silent for a moment.

Finally, the patience Faith and BJ gave each other on the line seemed to warm and revive the connection they felt through knowing Bill. BJ broke the silence and asked, using the Hebrew name for the booklet of Passover, "Please send me a digital copy of the *haggadah*."

* * *

At the next Adoption Triad Circle meeting Faith looked around the room. Susan wasn't there this time. She saw Clay. He had a full crown of white hair above chiseled good looks and long limbs. Who could miss him? She thought he presented well; a few blocks over on Broadway they'd call it *stage presence* and a few avenues up at Rockefeller Center, broadcasters would call it both camera-friendly and *gravitas*. He would always satisfy that "good fit" requisite demanded in corporate settings in a way shorter men, non-blonde women and others had to work hard to attain.

She noticed over the two years he had been coming to the adoption triad group that his instincts were to attack —the cheap joke of mimicry when someone stuttered or spoke too softly. But his reptilian brain at least was picking up that these effortless jabs he hadn't managed to shake from corporate life were making him unpopular here. It was only at a meeting six months in that Faith saw something miraculous. She wasn't sure others in the room caught it.

It was when Priscilla, a shy adoptee, fairly new to search, asked him something. Clay was in the middle of summing up about the latest stage of his search, "...she was friendly and all, my ex-girlfriend, reminiscing about our three years together. But when I asked the adoptive mother about her daughter, our daughter, she just clammed up."

Faith saw Priscilla lean forward as soon as Clay paused.

"You found the adoptive mother?" Priscilla asked.

Clay sneered, "Are you deaf or something? I can't even find out the adoption agency from the birth-mother."

"But I was confused because –"

"I'd say you're a little confused –"

"– because you said '*adoptive*' mother instead of '*birth*' mother."

"Nah."

Faith interjected, "Prissy's right, I heard '*adoptive*,' too."

But it was too late. Priscilla's cheeks were staining pale crimson and she was folding and refolding a sheet of paper in her lap until it was a small triangle.

Habitually smug, self-absorbed Clay sat mid thought, his mouth open and his eyes unfocused but alert, like a locksmith who has just heard a tumbler click before a door opens.

A few minutes later during the meeting break, Faith noticed Clay walk straight over to Priscilla, who had already stepped out into the hall. He leaned over her, each of them resting a shoulder against the paneled wall. It wasn't romantic, though it reminded Faith of couples at mixers. It struck her as fatherly, avuncular. He was talking and Priscilla's face was regaining its composure.

By the time the two co-facilitators called through the room door to reassemble, Clay had Priscilla laughing.

Faith noted that this wouldn't benefit his own search, therefore it was an unusual expenditure of energy for him. Clay was talking to meek Priscilla privately and therefore it wasn't even a performance for the others to see, to burnish his image.

He had just focused on making a withdrawn, "ordinary" stranger, feel better. For Clay, Priscilla wasn't a means to an end. Her hurt feelings mattered and doing right by her *was* the end. Maybe the world was becoming a more spacious, inhabited space than the narrow place where he had been living, his addiction to his career, his self-interest. A mousy stranger mattered now, too.

Over time, Faith noticed that if things got a little slow with his own search, he seemed to cop a thrill from watching another searcher's enthusiasm. His commitment to attending these meetings offered a relief to Faith who hoped to find good in her own birth-father, Bill Yard, whom she would meet in a few days.

Clay would reassure adoptees, "Okay, I waited decades to search but I promise you if my firstborn had shown up before then I would have agreed to meet. Anytime. Anywhere. But until three years ago..." His voice drifted a little but he was still leaning in, "...I guess it was about moving on and not dwelling on a defeat. Then when it started to gnaw at me, I told myself that I 'didn't have the right' to search. Maybe this is when the doors of the world started to open. First I was on one side thinking 'I don't have the right'...."

Faith caught Clay sliding a soft glance at Priscilla the first time he said something like this, "Today I realize I'm on the other side, Priscilla, thinking, 'I may or may not have a right *but* he or she *does*. My kid has the right to find me if they want. They have the right to demand that I look them in the eye," Clay paused before continuing, "I made one bad decision years ago; I don't need to let it make the rest of my life."

Faith and Priscilla both released their breath at the same time. They both heard what had just happened here. Not everyone else had. The gates had swung open for Clay and he could step through lightly.

~ 5 ~

SUSAN 2023, NEW JERSEY

The array of boxes, molded trays and plastic sheathed lab equipment in front of Susan reminded her of a first-generation pregnancy test. But the instructions that unfolded like an accordion switched her to another image. This shrink-wrap bore more than a passing resemblance to an ovulation test kit. Both kinds of kits just emphasized that no, you weren't going to get your descendants or heritage the straightforward way like everyone else did: by bearing or growing up with your own blood kin. For better or worse, descendants and ancestors were your own native fauna and human habitat for most people. Not her. She sighed. She dangled the directions for the DNA test kit at eye level. Its complexity was adding insult to injury.

She spat into a test tube. Resentment. Extra effort. Pain. *Am I ready to accept if I find nothing? Am I ready to have new people in my life if I'm welcomed? Am I supported enough, licked enough bad habits, and cultivated enough good habits to face a rejection? How will I take care of myself if, after a brief reunion, I am then ghosted?* Once the saliva reached the level mark, she snapped the lid shut with relief. It wasn't presto like the pregnancy kits with their pink or blue lines after a two-minute wait. Instead, she waited for her laptop to fire up so she could fill out field after field to register.

Next, she found her assigned code on the box and typed it into one of the data fields. She attached the right labels, the correct seals, and went outside to put the deck-of-cards-sized package into the mail. Once back inside, she placed the slip of paper printed with a twenty-five-digit key code into her top drawer so she could use it to access the results online once they were ready. When the email arrived one morning that enveloped the link to her results, Susan half inhaled, half shrieked before calling, "David!"

"Coming. Are you okay, Suzie?"

"They found over two hundred cousins, David."

Missing relatives. Their eyes locked knowingly. It was one of their—topics.

His shirt was untucked over charcoal sweatpants that few men's hips and thighs could fill as trimly as his did. Since their first meeting years ago in college, his once red hair had deepened to the color of gingersnap. From the birth of their first child, Lily, through their twins Noam and Maya who were about ten or so, she and David co-parented well. They had also remained lovers.

Susan saw him for the first time outside class in the campus student lounge. He was captain of their Division

I lacrosse team. It was a Sunday. Sylvie and she had their notes from that class, Clashing Myths in German Civilization, spread out in front of them.

"He's looking at you, Suzie," her roommate nudged.

"Probably one of those jocks who spends four years, or maybe the rest of their lives, being arrogant jerks," Susan decided to forget him and turned her eyes back to her notes.

"Then he'd be taking a gut class, not," Sylvie gestured at the books and CDs on the table in front of them, "not anything that requires you to listen to all eight hours of Wagner's *Ring des Nibelungen*. Herr Hansen is a sadist."

"Please don't plant any unwanted S & M images of Professor Hansen in my mind," Susan wanted to get off this subject, "Remember for the exam the opera ends on an unresolved E minor."

"Excuse me," it was David himself, "I'm thinking that would tie into Nietzsche's contention in 'The Tragedy of Wagner' that Wagner was using music, in this case the unresolved E, to create longing and unrealizable expectations in his audiences. Do you think that's reading too much into it?"

Susan found herself answering the jock who was now crouching down so they didn't have to strain to look up at him, "No, I think you're right. Wagner meant it to be manipulative."

David's dark red hair had a slight wave to it, and he was one of those people who had eyes that managed to pull off both intelligent and kind at the same time. But looks could be deceiving, Susan reminded herself. He seemed to sense the chill she was giving off. He turned and was now answering a question her roommate had thrown at him. As if it were the most natural thing in the world, the three of them ended up studying Clashing Myths in German Civilization together.

After a while Susan had to admit, without even seeing him on the field, why his teammates would choose him team captain. From his broad, relaxed shoulders to his pleasantly deep voice, there was something reassuring about being with him. He came across as book strong but not pretentious, athletic but not muscle bound. Most amazing of all, when her friend went to get a Tab to bring back to their room, David asked Susan if she would like to meet up again later for supper.

She found herself answering, "Yes."

* * *

They smiled with nostalgia still whenever thinking about their courtship. But there was a rough fissure between them when it came to how they viewed their own parents. In the subterranean layer that underlies every marriage, simmering magma, rock-scraping shifts, and rumbles were felt but remained unspoken. The discovery of David's long missing father briefly stripped their marriage bare. David's father had vanished when David was four. David's mother pretty much raised two boys alone, with the help of David's paternal uncles. David made do until Susan decided to search for her missing birth-mother, and up until the day the family got the call about a wildfire in Maine.

It took a blueberry field burn gone out of control to reveal to David and her brother-in-law Jonathan where their missing father had been. Susan had already visited her birth-country by then. David's reunion was not the one that hers was – of silks and curries and elephant rides. It was stripped down to a ruined cabin floor on which they found the charred human dust of his father.

Ever since his father left David and Jonathan and their mother in his rearview mirror, he'd been living up there on a plantation, what people in the north woods called a logging settlement. He had been alive and well—living with another woman—all throughout David's childhood and new fatherhood. The man himself had chosen to stay hidden. It was the fire that brought David and Jonathan some answers, but only after first snatching their father away.

David and Susan both expected to have a perfect fight, either during the long drive back after viewing the re-mains or later that night. Something about his father or something about her birth-father whom, at that time, she had never met. She had visited her birth-country only to realize that some losses are for keeps. But in the language of plate tectonics, the strains eased, the fissure finally mended itself. They talked; they were both good people. Any lava quickly crusted and became sparkling igneous bedrock paving a new way between them. They both shared loss—how simple it was to say that now. But they shared so much else.

Susan would learn that a few cultures still practiced clearing harvested fields with fire through controlled burns. Susan saw her first controlled burn when she visited her birth-country, Thailand, and saw that tapioca fields were cleared and nutrients returned to the soil through deliberately set fires. Tapioca was only one such crop. She learned from a Hawaiian friend that pineapple was another. In places like New England and the Maritime Provinces the technique was sometimes called swailing, an old Anglo-Saxon term long since abandoned on the British Isles, still used for the blueberry crop, like that one controlled burn that somehow became uncontrolled, taking the life of David's father and a couple dozen other souls.

Susan saw that "tapioca fire" after driving north from Bangkok with an interpreter guide and approaching the village of Ban Naan. They arrived in a haze of smoke something like, she imagined, a magician appearing from behind a dry ice machine. On the other side was her birth-mother's village, the family home, their reunion. As Susan lived it, searching for birth-family, visiting a birth-country, or having a reunion were all ways to clear and nourish ourselves, like a tapioca fire.

So it was no surprise now when David turned to her matter-of-factly after the DNA test and said what was between them, "Two hundred cousins means you're on the trail of your father. We're in this together. I've got your back, Susan."

She would need him.

The results did show hundreds of cousins but almost all turned out to be distant cousins. She learned that this meant many were connected seven or more generations ago. In other words, she shared a common ancestor two-hundred and fifty years or so earlier with some of these "cousins". It was a start but a slow one.

She worked like she always did. Reached out for allies and they were there. She knew genealogy sleuths from the adoption reform movement but she didn't have enough to go on for them to help yet.

The next three weeks she plunged into the world of online DNA. She found a project specifically for East and Southeast Asian adoptees. Some plans considered American Indians a branch of Asia, as did the two museums she was working with for a curatorial assignment. One recent contract was for a museum in Beijing that was called expansively "Hall of the Chinese People". There was another one in Nikko, Japan called "Hall of the Asian Peoples," where she attended the opening years earlier, around the time her first baby, Lily, was born. It was from there that she made her very first trip to her birth-country, her first trip to anywhere in Southeast Asia for that matter.

The technicalities confused Susan. There didn't seem to be a perfect correlation between percentage of shared DNA and closeness of relationship. There were things called segments, whatever they were, that determined physical traits. It seemed like twenty-three chromosomes had spawned twenty-three DNA discussion communities online.

She did find two silver needles in the DNA haystack: two second cousins. One never wrote back and she wondered why someone would take these tests in the first place if not to fill in the family tree. Susan thought in her case the family tree was turning out to be a stunted digital shrub.

The second cousin who did write back was a woman out in Oklahoma who was eager to compare notes – at first.

* * *

Susan emailed her own phone number to the cousin, who called her a few days later. Susan decided it would be better to tell her by telephone instead of email that she had been adopted out of their family. The kids were awake but David was home, so Susan was able to close the door and have the delicate conversation in the bedroom.

But when Susan couldn't provide any family surnames on her own side the cousin became suspicious. "Listen, I don't have any money for you, if that's what you're after. I'm not going to give out any addresses and I'm thinking I need to warn my family that you may be a scammer."

The hairs on Susan's arms stood up. She swallowed once and decided to share what she knew about her birth-father, "I think my father was a GI in Vietnam."

"What was his name?"

"I don't know, I think I said that before—I apologize—but I don't have dogtags or anything. Remember you and I found each other through the DNA company."

"Are you one of those Amerasians?"

Susan felt the warmth drain from her face and her fingers holding the device felt weak. She hated that term. She didn't know where to begin unpacking it. It made it sound like all GIs were black or white. Surely there were GIs from other backgrounds during that entire war. It lumped all people from an area larger than Europe and the Middle East into one category: Asia.

This cousin's question, "Are you one of those __?" echoed with generations of othering people like Susan who were caught at the interface of ethnicities.

Susan shook it off and answered, "Y-yes, I am. One more thing: he may or may not know I exist."

"You sure have some story there. I wish you luck, but I just can't see giving out contact information for my family."

Susan pointed out with alarm, "But the test you signed up for shows *us* - you and me - as cousins too."

Her new found cousin acted as though Susan hadn't spoken and continued, "Maybe one of them will sign up for the DNA testing service too, then when their results come in you can talk to them yourself."

"But –"

"It's really not my place, I'd never forgive myself if this weren't on the up and up. Just have patience. If you're meant to meet you will."

Susan exhaled. She had one last angle, "Could you ask them to take a test? I would be willing to pay for it."

She hadn't run this by David as a new line in the family budget—ninety-nine dollars a kit—but surely the knowledge would be worth the expense. She could look later for a sale somewhere online.

The stranger hesitated but wouldn't budge. "I'm not comfortable with money changing hands. I can certainly suggest they test. I'll even mention I found someone who came up as a second cousin. I'm not willing to promise more. Honey, if it's meant to be it will be. I'll see what I can do within reason."

Susan forced herself to thank the woman before hanging up. She was so frustrated she felt tears gathering in her eyes. She could fit in a twenty-five-minute run.

Twenty minutes later she was back, smiling to herself, and as she unlaced her shoes said to no one in particular, "It's time to call on Faith."

* * *

Faith listened to Susan run through her list of worries about working so hard for nothing, about not feeling entitled to contact genetic family, about being crazy, and then Faith cut her off.

"There's a song I always think was written for genealogists and family historians." Susan took the phone off speaker and put it to her ear. This was one of their things, sharing lyrics.

Faith then began to hum before singing the words to an old classic rock song, "Empty Pages" by the British band Traffic. *Staring at empty pages, centered 'round the same old plot / Staring at empty pages, flowing along the ages.... / Found someone who can comfort me, but there are always exceptions / And she's good at appearing sane, but I just want you to know.*

Then Faith paused.

"'She's good at appearing sane'? Faith. Really?" asked Susan.

"ARE sane. That's what I meant to say. You're not crazy, you're sane for wanting to work through all the empty pages, filling in the blanks of your story. It's a '*same old plot*': the hero, who is an orphan, an adopted person, or a donor-conceived person searching for their origins, but it's retold with every generation, '*flowing along the ages*'. You are cool, and sane and doing the right thing. Because you and others are searching, it makes it easier for me to search."

Susan leaned back into the cushion of the sofa she was sitting on before asking, "Because you have a friend who really 'gets' you, right?"

"Yes."

"Faith, do you know the Lou Reed song 'Perfect Day'?

"No," answered Faith.

Susan said, "It was written by Lou Reed after he left Velvet Underground, B side of 'Walk on the Wild Side'. His version was on the soundtrack of *Trainspotting* but I liked the Chris Whitley version on *Gaz Bar Blues*."

"How do you even know a movie called *Gaz Bar Blues*?" asked Faith.

"David," Susan said.

Her husband loved the Quebec and Halifax cultural scenes, not as precious or pressured as some of the Brooklyn and Manhattan island clutch, lively and warmer. He was from Maine; it was a Maine thing. Enough winter nights and you could learn more dot-alt music and movies than an old time New York City clubber ever had the time to.

Susan continued, "He downloaded the movie from a Montreal art cinema site. The only part I remember goes something like this. This is my back at ya, sweet Faith-friend:

Just a perfect day
You made me forget myself
I thought I was someone else
Someone good"

"Aww, Susan. I make you feel 'like someone good'? What do you mean you had to 'forget yourself'? You are one of the best people I know. By the way," Faith leaned forward with mischief in her eyes, "I do know that song. It was on the trailers for season three of *Downton Abbey*."

Something in Susan relaxed as they both laughed.

~ 6 ~

FAITH 2023, NEW JERSEY

Faith tapped in a number. It rang and she waited for Susan to pick up. As life built up its collection of relationships and betrayals, as Faith's standards of trustworthiness became clear, she had come to value Susan's friendship more and more. They confided in each other, cared about each other's aging adoptive parents, and helped each other in their searches for their birth-parents.

Faith's heart raced with the thought that something Clay said could be another "tapioca fire". Maybe Clay Dennen with his new project of search and reunion for military birth-fathers could help them set another tapioca fire that would clear away underbrush, cleanse the ground.

Faith heard Susan pick up, they exchanged a few catch ups, and then Faith started in with, "You haven't been to the circle recently. There're the usual genealogy search specialists you can reach out to. But here's something new: there's a man in the group, a birth-father, who's starting to work on searches tied to members of the armed forces. Clarence Dennen—he goes by Clay—do you remember him? I don't know if you knew he had a career in the Navy before he transitioned into the executive suite. That might be what you need to find your American birth-father."

"I remember him. His number is on the Adoption Triad Circle roster that just went out but I never see him. On the other hand, I don't always get to meetings. Isn't he also the one who got Tony Silvio on board to testify for Ted Landtsman's heritage equality case?" said Susan.

"Yes, that's him!" said Faith, "Clay may know of a way to match someone stationed in Thailand, or stationed in Vietnam on leave in Thailand, to your birth-father. The reason you don't see Clay much is he's busy reaching out to other birth-fathers who served in the military and he leads the group who've agreed to be witnesses. He'll be at the adoption *seder*, which goes out in next week's announcements. I'm calling you before..."

"Don't you have enough to keep all that free time filled? After a full-time job and three kids?" said Susan.

"I could do this forever. Most of my work happens after the kids' bedtimes. Closed adoptions usually and anonymous donations are unnecessary secrets that play out through the generations. You know this," said Faith, "If there's one thing I do that matters, aside from being a parent, this is it, Susan. Bringing about reunions."

"Uh-huh," Susan agreed, then added, "We can't force relationships, I get that. But at least once everyone deserves a reunion."

* * *

Faith and her mother, Carolyn Givvers, understood each other aesthetically in a way no one else in the family did. Despite ups and downs, Faith found herself choosing to move nearby to her parents when she returned from Japan and they planned all holidays together. Faith and her mother were in and out of each other's homes. Their lives were filled by work and her young children. But Faith's adoptive mother died too soon from the same cancer that forced her to have the hysterectomy in her twenties.

After her mother died, Faith's adoptive father stunned her by withdrawing from both fatherhood and grandfatherhood. A woman who tried to seduce him unsuccessfully a couple times while her mother was alive moved in rapidly. Although Faith's father had rejected the woman repeatedly in the past, he succumbed now. Faith remembered him swearing under his breath several times on the day of the wedding to his new wife, although she'd never heard him swear before. They often bickered. It didn't feel like love, but fear of being alone.

Within weeks of the wedding his new wife insisted that Faith and her sister only communicate with their father through her. Dad got this wife to back down for a while, but regular family Sunday dinners were a thing of the past. Then the wife, not satisfied at partial domination, insisted he disown the grandchild who was named after his first wife – and he obeyed – even though the cutie was only seven years-old at the time. None of the extended Givvers family showed the courage to resist this woman; they claimed to be staying neutral by excluding Faith and her children from family events while inviting her father and the new wife.

Families are complicated. Faith simplified it by loving her late mother fiercely and remembering her father for the man he was when her mother was still alive. At any rate, her Mom's small family stood by Faith, and she and Susan felt like soul mates.

SUSAN 2023, NEW YORK CITY & NEW JERSEY

The rest of Susan's household was downstairs watching a Harry Potter together (David noted Harry was an intra-family adoptee) while Susan coiled happily on a chez in the living room. She found the chez at a Salvation Army sale and had just re-finished the wood herself, inspired by planning an exhibit about the 20th century American crafts movement.

This program would be particularly cool because her friend Faith's adoptive mother, Carolyn Givvers, was listed in the American crafts movement collection of the Smithsonian Art Institute's Renwick Gallery. Susan had photos of Carolyn's jewelry fanned across the carpet in front of her.

Most of the pieces were plexiglass "pectoral art" that draped over a model's shoulders and covered her chest like a breastplate. Faith's mother credited a color theory class with Josef Albers for the inspiration to let translucent layers of colors play and move together in her pectoral art. The Smithsonian owned several pieces like this but one piece was different and Susan asked Faith about it once.

It, as Faith explained to Susan, was the most personal jewelry her mother ever made, the handmade silver filigree cradling a gift of washed glass from Faith. Faith remembered that as a little girl she had found the sea glass one summer on a walk along the ocean-bound granite ledges of Haystack Mountain School of Crafts in Maine.

"I was so proud to give this treasure to Mom. What do you suppose it was?"

Susan guessed, "Its contours make it most likely from a crystal pitcher."

"I was so happy when she turned it into part of the pendant for the silver necklace. Despite that love, maybe because of it, my father's wife wanted the silver and sea glass necklace to go, like she was erasing the mother and child who came before in his life."

Susan shuddered when she remembered Faith telling her that the wife also insisted that it *not* go to Faith.

Faith's adoptive father shocked everyone by giving in. Instead he found a compromise between letting Faith keep it and having it melted down for the silver. He would offer it to the Smithsonian. They accepted it with the description of a "sterling silver and found beach glass neckpiece" for its Renwick Gallery catalog.

For this exhibit though, Susan made sure to include the Kriegman *mise-en-scène* (Carolyn would have appreciated the French term better than "setting the scene") and photos of the actual Deer Isle shoreline where Faith walked.

* * *

Susan went to the top of the stairs to make sure David and the kids were still engrossed with the movie. Then taking a deep breath, Susan punched Clay's number on her smartphone and as she waited for Clay to answer, she wondered where her backstory would lead.

Clay was more thoughtful than Susan's few impressions of him had led her to expect. In fact, he was eager to help and could tick off over a dozen favors or searches other than his own that the Birth-Fathers' Club had gotten him involved in. Susan asked how his own search was going.

"Nothing new. Well, the latest thing is that Fred did ask me the name of the attorney who packaged the adoption. I couldn't remember it, Susan. Then he read off a list of attorneys who were known to work in adoption back at that time, that region. One rang a bell. Fred went to locate him but turns out he died almost a decade ago."

"How disappointing, Clay. I'm really sorry."

"That doesn't change a thing I'm doing. If I stop, then they've won. If I can still help someone else, then we're winning. Let's see what we can do to help you."

* * *

It only took two weeks before Clay was back in touch, catching Susan in the kitchen on a morning she was working remotely. He sounded almost mellow over the phone in his new role as a genealogy search specialist. There was a reverence as Clay read from his notes.

"For service at Ap Tan Hoa, Republic of Vietnam on May twenty-first, nineteen sixty-nine he received the Distinguished Service Cross however, in lengthy affidavits submitted by nearly a dozen fellow soldiers, mostly self-described 'country boys' from the South and Midwest, he should have been nominated for the even higher Medal of Honor previous to this for his service in Tam Ky, Vietnam. There on March sixth and seventh of the same year, he secured a needed route of retreat for his rifle company by single-handedly defending a hill for twenty-four hours against waves of North Vietnamese soldiers.

"However, an anti-Semitic sergeant named Arthur Hilmers consistently 'volunteered' him for the most dangerous patrols and missions and refused orders to fill out the nominating paperwork for the Medal of Honor. Despite this, your birth-father returned for a second tour."

"Wow. Did he come back alive after that?" Susan asked. She felt like she would weep if the answer were no. Her father, dead, as a young man.

Clay must have slipped back into his uniformed days. He answered, "Affirmative."

Susan felt her eyes tearing with relief. "Where is he now? Was he injured in Vietnam?"

She could hear Clay ruffling through his notes before he read, "He currently resides in Deerfield Beach, Florida. Retired."

She felt a rush of adrenaline like the last leg of a track race. "Do you know his name? I can't wait to hear his name, Clay."

Clay chuckled at Susan's enthusiasm. She heard him clear his throat. "Susan, it's Master Sergeant Solomon Leonard Morris, US Army, Retired. He prefers to go by 'Sol'."

Immediately a thought caught in the back of Susan's mind. It sounded like the phone call went well, but if it hadn't, might Clay be the only one – and not her – to speak with Sol? To at least hear her father's voice? She decided to keep any disappointment to herself.

"You spoke to him already?"

"I called his voicemail and his message said 'Sol'. You ready? He did call me back and I let him know who I am, that he's got a daughter, and just a little about you, that you're well. He is open to being contacted by you. I've got his phone number right here."

Susan copied it down, speechless. She rushed her thank-yous to get Clay off the phone so she could call her birth-father. Then she carried her device and small notepad into the living room where she picked the most comfortable chair to perch on.

She mis-typed and started over, then worried she'd

typed the precious number wrong again, so she hung up before it could ring through. Finally, as though pressing the raised soft squares on the keypad were a religious rite, she entered the number sequence gingerly to summon her paternal ancestor.

She swallowed as the phone rang. It clicked and then a voice began speaking in a warm baritone. Her heartbeat picked up and she was flooded with a warm affection, and then almost immediately had a realization that made her shoulders slump with disappointment and, yes, relief. She was only listening to a recording. She hung up.

His voice stayed in her ears though.

She stood up from the upholstered chair and took a walk three times around the coffee table. She'd chosen to call from the living room instead of any other room because it was the prettiest. The coffee table was elegant but simple and because it had been her mother's she remembered it from childhood. There were cut flowers from a neighbor in a crystal vase on the mantel. The midmorning the sun slanted through the beveled windows at just the right angle to splash rainbows across the wooden floor. The one rug at the foot of the sofa was from a curating assignment she had loved, in all her favorite colors. As she paced, barefoot, on its fibers she noticed that that each circle around the table took seven steps. Seven steps in three circles, Susan felt it might somehow be auspicious and decided to call back.

This time, she listened with gratitude instead of fear to the deep straightforward voice. This was the man whom all the unwritten rules said not to ask about. This was the man who had the power to matter whether he welcomed or rejected her.

The message tone seemed to come too soon. Susan inhaled and then mentioned Phuket and described the resort island in case he didn't remember the name. She carefully left her American name, Susan Piper, and then felt a little daring.

"Sol, you should also know my birth-name in case it has some significance to you. It was *Suwan*," she said, before gently disconnecting the call.

* * *

When he did call about an hour or so later, she realized that he must feel the same about long phone conversations as she did. Rather than share much on the phone, he pretty much let it be known, in a not unfriendly way, that he would take a DNA test himself just to confirm.

Sol then added something Susan thought was pretty perceptive, and kind.

"You and I have a hunch already that it's true. That we're related. A DNA test will make it easier for the rest of the kinfolk to accept."

Kinfolk. Before Susan could completely digest the reality of his maybe introducing her to more relatives, she found herself riffing with Sol on childhood memories of that holiday from the Book of Esther, Purim. As though that weren't exciting enough, her birth-father launched into the logistics of his driving up from Florida to meet her in New York City.

Then he ambled into talking about visiting Oklahoma on the way. Is Oklahoma on the way? She wasn't going to argue, didn't want to jinx it. By the end of the call her heart was pounding and Sol had made online hotel reservations off one of the avenues for the middle of next week. He wasn't staying for long and that made her spirits sink a little. She almost imagined herself pleading in a little-girl voice, "No, Daddy, stay, stay longer," and then realized a long weekend might be too much of a good thing for either of them. Before Susan and Sol hung up, they exchanged emails and both promised to upload and send photos.

* * *

Fast forward: Susan got there first and asked for a booth in the back. The booth, the walls, and the narrow hanging lamps were all oranges and browns. It was a good, cozy place to meet. A few minutes later she saw him come through the door and recognized him right away. He walked straight toward her. It was a brisk walk, just like you'd expect from someone who served his life in the armed forces.

"Hello!" Sol said.

She stood and stepped out of the booth to say, "Hello, I feel a little dizzy with the unreal-ness of meeting my birth-father. It's nice to meet you."

"Susan," he gave her shoulder a squeeze and they sat down.

She couldn't compare him to her adoptive father who had actually raised a child, her. That wouldn't be fair. She noticed that his ears looked less like hers than her adoptive dad's did. Her dad was less muscular than Sol but slightly taller and she realized she never looked for physical similarities with her dad before. She looked for them with Sol. It's all she had.

Right off she noticed his hands. Something about them reminded her of Lily's and her own, even though he was a man. She thought some more of her three kids and tried to sift our what of their features, their movements and gestures, reminded her of images of Noklek, what came from David's family, and what might have come from this man before her. Her son Noam might have his or David's larger frame. She and both Lily and Maya had narrower shoulders and flatter rib cages. His military career, of course, brought to mind David's older brother, Jonathan, who would probably be U.S. Coastguard for life. Wait – that wasn't genetic, she reminded herself and then drew a blank. Maybe, just maybe, there was a timbre to Sol's voice that predicted what Noam's would grow into but she couldn't be sure.

Her birth-father was attentive, making sure they got refills on the water and rose to get salt and pepper shakers missing from their table. He answered her questions. She had prepared a list on her phone to be sure the most important ones were asked in case this was their last meeting. Funny, because by the end she thought they both knew this was just their first meeting. In fact, even though she felt a little shy about it...shy? Yes, but she made a judgement call and despite her reticence Susan invited him to the online gathering in the works with Faith.

She thought about Faith's reunion with Bill and hoped Sol wouldn't become as layered as Faith's birth-father turned out to be.

8

SOLOMON 2024, FLORIDA

Susan invited me to our first meeting, up there in New York. Now, for our second meeting, I am here in Florida, alone but connected. I log onto Zoom from the coffee table in the living room and there is my Susan. She and her group have been hosting these search and reunion seders for a couple of years.

One frame is a wide angle shot of the two dozen or so people gathered in person. They sit around a U-shaped configuration of tables set with flowers. Susan told me on our last call that people would bring them from their own gardens. Daffodils bloom from several vases. Behind the seated people, I make out easels pinned with what might be meeting announcements and sign-up sheets for members of the adoption groups in attendance.

Susan already told me no other birth-fathers would be at the in-person dinner but there might be others on Zoom. When each person introduces themselves and where they are from I realize the gathering is mostly adult adoptees and donor-conceived people, adoptive and recipient parents, and birth-mothers. There are a few couples, as well as social workers from New Jersey, New York and Pennsylvania and a smattering from New England. They haven't started yet so I exchange pleasantries with Susan and several people react. *They must know about our reunion.*

The invitation emailed to everyone ahead of time asked us to have an object from our adoption story. At first, I thought about my dog-tags. I'll slip them on right now. Feel cool, nice with the AC shut off. I also could have used my plane tickets from the visit to New York with Susan, but I threw them out when I got back and realized I need, will have, more visits. This reunion isn't a one-time event. I'm not sure what kind of relationship I want. I'm not her parent, but she is my daughter in a sense. I don't want to be in touch with her birth-mother, Noklek, I mean if she showed up, I'd take them both out to dinner but I just don't see it. I'd take her adoptive father out to dinner too, or let him pay, whichever made him feel better, follow his lead on that one. She told me about her mother passing. Doesn't sound like he's much involved now that he's remarried though: amazing.

The table looks like the basics you'd expect, six foods, each representing part of the story of the Exodus. Susan is explaining about *afikomen* and *tsafun*, the part I loved as a kid, bet she did too. She explains how *tsafun* means search in Hebrew and it comes at the end of the *seder* meal. *Seder* means 'order' or choreography of this holiday.

They're setting it up now by breaking a matzah in half, setting one piece back on a plate of matzahs and covering them, and then Susan hands the other piece, the *afikomen*, to an older woman. That woman, with a twinkle in her eye, hams it up holding a posterboard that says:

I hide your *afikomen*=origins.
I am a:
a) social worker
b) adoption attorney
c) fertility clinic

The *afikomen* lady mugs for the camera before disappearing offscreen to hide the matzah. A man with a gravelly voice begins reading from the *haggadah*, "....A *haggadah* is the traditional booklet for the celebration of Passover that recounts Moses' leading the Exodus out of Egypt. Also contained in a *haggadah* are psalms, prayers, and rituals. They all act like synapses that make the main story that much more deeply felt...."

I don't have my own copy of the *haggadah* so I put my screen on speaker view and flick a glance toward the Florida room where the sun's setting rays are pouring across the calm air. I excuse myself by holding up a finger, get up, and go to the kitchen. We usually use four glasses of wine as part of the story, so I uncork and pour myself a glass. I carry it and the rest of the bottle back with me to the living room and set them a safe distance from the keyboard.

Now a man with a giant gold cross in his collar is reading. *Ah, an interfaith gathering.*

"...We're grateful that for many of us the story of our adopted religion is the story of severance and search. It can resonate for us whether our families are transracial, international, set in open or closed adoptions, and we welcome our newest participants from the donor-conceived community.

"What we've done is add stories, (or in Hebrew, *midrashim*) to the original story in the Bible. Some of the *midrashim* come from the Talmud, some come from the historian Josephus, and some are based on the feelings that are companions to a relinquishment or a search and reunion with DNA relatives.

"In the case of donor-conceived people, DCPs....'"

"DCPs", never heard that before.

"I want to make a quick aside here: *midrashim* have a very long tradition in Jewish life, as a way to elaborate on puns in a text, to give names to the unnamed or to explain inconsistencies. To give you an example, it's said in the Bible that Moses preferred to speak to Pharaoh and the Hebrews through an intermediary from his birth-family, his brother Aaron. The rabbis came up with a *midrash* that explained Moses' reticence by saying that Moses was a stutterer. So later, when we go around the table taking turns reading from this text, if you'd rather not read aloud or if you stutter over a line, you should remember that you are following in the tradition of Moses."

I chuckle.

Next Susan calls on Clay, the Navy man who brought us together. *Clay sure doesn't look Jewish, hah ha.* Of course, it's not a Jewish group anyway.

Clay begins reading, "The biblical Moses was born a Hebrew, raised as an Egyptian, and married into the tribe of Midianites. Thus, he can serve as an archetype for anyone who is trying to synthesize the two (or more) selves of a variegated background. Different readers of the story of Moses will bring different meanings to the metaphors 'Egyptian' and 'Hebrew.'

"For people who rediscover spirituality as Moses did, the word 'Egyptian' may mean their secular side while 'Hebrew' symbolizes their religious side.

"For people who emigrate as Moses did, 'Egyptian' may represent the people of their birth-country and 'Hebrew' may represent the people of their Promised Land.

"For people who have an extended family of many faiths, 'Egyptian,' 'Midianite', and 'Hebrew' may each mean family to them. For many around this table and online, like Moses, 'Egyptian' means adoptive home and 'Hebrew' means genetic heritage.

"In the *midrash* we learn that the Exodus included both Hebrews and Egyptians journeying together and in this version of the Exodus story, not all the non-Jews are bad guys. More later...."

I recognize all the traditions, the symbolic food. It is interesting how Susan and her friends give each a new twist. Something here. Companionship radiates from this group, like a hum. Eventually the highlighted square on the screen goes to a man who introduces himself as Paul, an "anonymous donor". Paul shares that his DNA son found him through a fifty-dollar DNA test kit. Paul adds that he himself had never taken a genetic test but a second cousin had.

That's all it took? Huh.

Paul begins a section on how it feels different to be a Moses, a donor-conceived or adopted person, without "heritage equality". I know that is what the Birth-Fathers' Club witnesses are about. Susan hasn't asked yet but I wouldn't be surprised if she asks me to testify or do one of those depositions or whatnot. I think it's in one of the courts of appeals, she said. I honestly don't know what I'd say, what they'd need me to say. I keep listening as the screen switches to a college student with pronouns they/them.

This is a lot to take in but I think I understand. I was raised with most of my family in the same county, except for some up in Chicago. I always took that for granted. I never really imagined what an adoptee, an immigrant, or any other kind of searcher felt. Good for Susan, taking the initiative.

"Eventually I found many of us, hiding in plain sight. The most famous are the twinned founders of Rome, Romulus and Remus, improbably raised by a she-wolf, and Moses, raised by the daughter of the same Pharaoh who originally ordered the death of all male Hebrew infants like Moses!

"Do we know her name? The rabbis of the Talmud

state that she is named *Batyah* or daughter of God for God adopted her just as she adopted Moses.

"Why was she at the Nile? The historian Josephus wrote that she went to nature, to the banks of the river, to soothe her pain at infertility.

"In both versions of the tale of the adoptee, the rescuer who becomes their protective adoptive parent could have been their most dangerous enemy. That they did not implies to me there is something conciliatory in the universe (God!) that leads people to do good despite traditional strictures of race, class, and in the case of Romulus and Remus, even species. (Similarly, the married, middle-class couples who might be expected to most object to unwed motherhood and illegitimacy are the ones most likely to become adopters.)

That is interesting. The civilizations of both Rome and Jerusalem.

Faith steps forward. Then bends down to say something conspiratorially to a couple who look like adoptive parents before she reads, "Adoptees begin their quest when they finally venture back to their origins. Romulus and Remus begin it when they return from the wild to the world of humans. Moses embarks on his when he hears the voice in the burning bush calling him away from Midian and back to Egypt, the land of his birth, adoption and childhood.

Faith passes it to the wife who turns a stapled page and reads, "For those of us working for adoptee and DCP heritage equality, we get a reminder that we're on the right side of history when God Themself undermines all the rules sealing, closing, amending, or redacting our heritage. God from the burning bush tells Moses the names of his paternal ancestors, declaring, 'I am the God of your fathers, Abraham, Isaac, and Jacob.'"

A few people laughed and clap, nodding.

After a pause, the prospective adoptive dad reads, "Like Moses, I returned to 'Egypt' only after becoming a parent and after living in a foreign country, Japan, that emphasized a shared history and 'race' as the basis of its polity. Immigrant countries like the U.S.A., on the other hand, are similar to adoptive families in their being bonded by affection and ideals, not blood."

Next someone on one of the video conference screens reads, "I wanted to celebrate the process of an adult adoptee's or immigrant's or convert's or spiritual seeker's search and reunion. Sometimes, of course, the end of a search does not lead to a reunion, but to a different resolution. I blended the biblical story of Moses with commentaries on it from the Talmud and my own insights as an adoptee."

The person in the next square reads, "At first recollection, the story of Moses may sound like an adoptive parent's worst nightmare: a Hebrew baby is adopted by the Egyptians only to grow up and kill the Egyptian Pharaoh. Then he runs off with the Hebrews, never to return to Egypt. But there are lesser-known commentaries that lend the story depth and compassion. For example, according to the Oral Tradition, Moses brings his adoptive mother and other Egyptians who opposed slavery with him when the Hebrews flee Egypt..."

Next, they begin to reenact the Ten Plagues just like I do every year at my sister's. Each square fills with a person reciting the English and Hebrew name for a plague as they dip their finger in their wine and sprinkle a drop on a side plate.

"...10. *Makat B'chorot*/Death of the Firstborn: Death of the hope for a biological child.

"It was the final plague, the death of the firstborn, that makes Moses' adoptive family understand. For Batyah, the adoptive mother, that firstborn was the biological child that infertility kept from her. Until she mourned her un-conceived, miscarried, aborted or stillborn child, Batyah could not empathize with Moses' longing for biological ancestors, a longing that was painfully similar to a longing for biological descendants...."

Huh, that same familiar sting. When I realized during my last break-up that the multi-year relationship that was dying was maybe my last chance at children. I thought I was over this, the sting, this lonesome sting of childlessness that returns randomly like a nerve pain. No, I'll tuck that up, I'm here now, I'll focus on this seder.

Susan's friend, Faith, is still reading, "Both Batyah and Moses, adopter and adoptee, shared a wish for a biological link from generation to generation. Pass. Helen?"

A woman named Helen appears in the speaker view

and introduces herself, "Helen from Morristown, adoptive mother here."

Helen has a warm, rich voice. She begins reading.

"Batyah not only came to understand her son Moses, she chose, like some other Egyptians, to join the *erev rav* or 'mixed multitude' that the Bible says follow Moses out of Egypt and across the Red Sea. Batyah did this from a mother's love, but also, perhaps, because she sensed that she would see her ethical will realized through Moses.

"And this is exactly what will happen. Moses follows the example set by his mother when she rescued him from the bulrushes. He goes on to teach the 'mixed multitude' that we must remember the widow, the orphan, and the stranger.

"Moses is remembering that he is tied to Batyah *not* by nature but by nurture, when he taught a new way for the Hebrews to see community and family. Whereas Abraham had introduced physical circumcision to bind them one to the other, Moses now taught them spiritual 'opening of the heart' to bind them together by love as it is meant in Deuteronomy 10:16 and Deuteronomy 30:16....

I drain my glass and pour another. Pretty soon a small group re-enacts the search, *tsafun*, and discovers the hidden matzah, *afikomen*. I get my dog-tags ready. Faith goes first.

"I've brought this photo album of my birth-family. I've also slid in the pressed flowers and hand-made prints my birth-mother sent from her home in Europe."

Next Susan pulls a small bolt of cloth out from next to

her seat. It's the nubby texture I remember from Thailand. Red silk in which gold, turquoise and emerald threads bob in and out. Next Susan even holds up what must be a picture of a now middle-aged Noklek. *I expect to recognize Noklek, but I don't honestly.*

Near the front of the room, I swear I see that performer with the rock memoir out, the one who reveals he's a birth-father, Tony Silvio. Why didn't they announce him or something?

Tony Silvio, if it is him, has a broad grin that seems to expand when it's his turn and everyone's eyes are on him. He casually just reaches to his side and gives the shoulder of the young woman next to him a squeeze. She breaks into a grin and reaches back for him too. Obviously, his birth-daughter. It's right there.

Many people have brought photographs, and one birth-mother has a picture of her son she cut out of a yearbook in a public library. Her son died several years ago, only a few months after trying unsuccessfully to contact her, yet the adoption agency and his adoptive parents refused to tell her the nature of his death or to share pictures of him.

Another birth-mother praised her son's parents and said the success of his adoption is one of the things that always keep her feeling optimistic.

One adoptee, Father Tom Brosnan, has a black and white picture of a biological uncle who not only shared the same first name, but is also a member of the priesthood.

An adoptive mother shows the home-made adoption

announcement they sent out after a five-year wait to adopt their foster son.

Many people brought poems they had written about adoption. One birth-mother brought two notebooks of poems.

Someone brought a drawing of a birth-mother floating Moses' cradle out into the bulrushes.

One adoptive mother shows a picture of her own mother who encouraged her to adopt in the first place.

One adoptee stands up and says that adoption has been a blessing and her reunion with her birth-parents now makes her feel doubly blessed.

Another adoptee whose search has been nothing but false leads and dead ends, introduces her daughter. Through her daughter she has found some of the continuity and sense of connection she could not find through searching.

It is a lot to take in. Everyone must feel the same because no one is in a hurry to pick up the *seder* booklet right away. The silence is companionable. Good people today. There is that hum, like I noticed at the beginning, of us just being together, like everything is going to be okay, or at least better.

After another moment, Faith picks up her *haggadah* to read. They go into a passage comparing Moses, Oedipus, and Elijah while I go back to the kitchen and spread some horseradish with beet juice on a matzah. The kick clears my sinuses.

Suddenly I hear everyone reading in unison and I bring my plate out to the living room.

"Malachi prophesies: 'Behold, I will send you Elijah the Prophet and he will turn the hearts of the parents to the children and the hearts of the children to the parents before the coming of the great and awesome day of God.'"

Powerful words. The room is silent for a moment before they close, name-checking Moses' birth-father, Amram, and the biblical 'male donor', Judah, from the story of Judah and Tamar with the last few lines of the *haggadah*.

Gives me an idea. No one really goes deep about Amram or Judah as fathers. Reminds me I signed up to give the Bible talk at our congregation's next lay-led prayer service. I don't know what I need to say yet about Amram and Judah, but maybe as I read the scripture it will come to me.

Part 3

From the FF documentary:

FAITH
"Oh, the climax of the search? It wasn't just meeting my birth-father. It was finding out through DNA testing that – well, we're going to show that later in the documentary, right? I won't give it away."

SOLOMON
"Feeling blessed that my daughter found her way to America, that a loving couple raised her, and that she found Noklek and that they brought each other peace; that's the high point of this reunion."

SUSAN
"What's the high point of my search and reunion? Going to his place in Florida even more than going to – sorry, Faith told me not to give that away yet *[laughs]*. I'll just say this: his agreeing to testify with the Birth-Fathers' Club made him a hero in my eyes."

~ 9 ~

BILL 2022, NEW YORK CITY

After the waitress leaves us alone at our table, I look down at my watch and pretend to adjust the time. I watch her taking in the pink walls that make all the diners look flushed. My breakfast companion and I sit alongside a wall-length, gilt-framed mirror. Full fluorescent moons glow from the ceiling through strings of glass beads, not quite chandeliers. The effect is an early twentieth century faux baroque. The chairs are dark wood sleigh-back and the tables a white linoleum set with paper placemats. Light, warm, twinkles the various edges of plates, tables, the chrome on the bus boy's folding server stand, despite this Manhattan space being down a flight of stairs.

Faith looks at me and says in an amused, playful voice, "You have tri-colored hair: salt-and-pepper interspersed with wisps of brown."

I don't think she means a takedown, so I reply by tightening my lips into a smile, "Calico. I am 'the cat that walked by himself'."

"Rudyard Kipling!"

I smile at her, then glance over at a waiter. When I look back at Faith, I ask, "So what do you want to know?"

For some reason, this question appears to startle her. It is appropriate, trite even in the world of search and re-union, I imagine. How many decades have I been hearing at my city government office about activists lobbying the state legislatures so they can have this moment?

I try to imagine what sitting across the table is like for this young woman. Hers is beyond intent listening. She seems to be taking in my face and eyes as much as my words. I feel her watch the way I lean forward over my plate to give an answer in a more discreet register. The way my arms and shoulders relax and I sit back, looking up, when our dishes arrive. Now she is looking at my torso and even lets out a laugh.

I'm unnerved that I already know the answer, but ask the question anyway, "What is it?"

"Um," her tone is still amused but apologetic, "We have the same rib cage. I hope this doesn't sound too personal, but the way you sighed when the food came..." she finishes the thought up quickly, "Torsos do open and close."

I try again to smile. I realize that nothing she does or says is going to allow me to relax so I swallow and tighten my grip on my tea cup without lifting it. The hand I keep safely out of view is trembling. My only goal will be to steady myself through this breakfast. I wish I feel what-ever it is I'm supposed to be feeling for this grown daugh-ter. Instead, all I sense is that swallowing will be hard. I wonder how many minutes have passed but I don't want to look at my watch just yet.

I hear her ask another question, "What's our background?"

I give her the mostly true answer, "Irish."

I look over her long loose hair that curls with colors like late summer seeds, auburn and chestnut intertwined. The smattering of freckles across the bridge of her nose and cheeks. Her coloring is more like mine. Ophelia's complexion was olive-toned. I continue, "An Irishman came from, probably, County Cork seven generations ago. Eight for you."

She doesn't miss a beat adding "Nine for my children." Then she proceeds to list each of them, names and ages.

I'm not ready for that. I recoil at the thought of grandchildren. I think of the Sorcerer's Apprentice, the version with Mickey Mouse as the apprentice, and its reproducing buckets: I screw up once and now the unintended and untended descendants keep multiplying.

I watch her pick up and weigh the smooth flatware in her left hand, then gamely plunge its tines into the cumulus of scrambled eggs, but she too refuses to react.

I listen to the sound of metal clicking against the thick china dinner plate, again realizing I should be offering more—emotion, information—and not wanting to.

She breaks the silence with "Where does the Italian come in? I remember my birth-mom saying she heard you describe big Italian Sunday suppers in Queens."

I guess my eyes must have looked doleful, or pitying. She and I had already established over the phone that I've never lived in Queens. It was Brooklyn. My father came there from Arkansas, leaving behind the Cherokee and Choctaw kin only to situate himself with Ma's family in a Mohawk enclave of North Gowanus, Brooklyn. Some called it Little Caughnawaga but today the Wigwam Bar and everything else is gone and they've renamed it Boerum Hill. The neighborhood was already changing by the time I met Ophelia. Maybe Ophelia didn't want Faith to find me. Tried to throw her with a futile campaign of misinformation. I look at her a minute.

"You're Irish and American Indian. The first Irishman came over, a trapper or a farmer in northern New York, and married an Iroquois. Mohawk, I think. Then there was my grandmother. She claimed to be a Cherokee, full-blooded, but my aunt said we were also Choctaw and have the relatives in Arkansas to prove it. So both sides of my family had Irish and Indian."

Faith laughs, and then making letter "I" with both her hands, says, "Guess it must have been the letter 'I' then: Italian, Irish, Indian."

I don't laugh.

Faith ignores this but adds, "Oh, did you ever hear about Robbie Robertson?"

"Frontman of The Band. Best man at Bob Dylan's wedding." This is a little more interesting to me.

Faith is trying to draw some connection. "Well, he had a birth-father, too, who was a card shark," she says, her eyes twinkling as though sharing personal gossip, "And his mother had grown up on the Six Nations Indian Reserve in Canada."

I pause and think about my rock memoir collection, think about mentioning it to Faith and how it's my way of reading about other birth-fathers. Instead, I put the thought aside: Robbie Robertson is not a birth-father, at least not that I know of.

After a moment more I continue stoically, "There were never big suppers and Ophelia was never invited to meet the family. My family's not close and she always met me at the studio. I think I met her mother and sister, Janice, once over the Jewish holidays. The mother and sister were both very petite, but not Ophelia," For an unnerving moment I remember the feel of Ophelia's shoulders, and add, "She'd been swimming a lot that summer and was really toned."

Faith passes me a basket of popovers. She asks, "Ophelia said you met at the old castle at the northern end of Manhattan—the Cloisters?"

"Yes, we did—it was a Saturday afternoon. I came there with a sketch pad. She was already set up with an easel and acrylic paints."

I came over and chatted Ophelia up a little in the afternoon and then went back to my own easel. It was when the light was low in the sky that she came over to look at what I had been doing: clutches of faces, visitors to the grounds. Before the sun set, we took a walk through the knot gardens high on a ridge overlooking the Hudson River on one side and the Bronx on the other.

I add, without a hint of nostalgia, "We talked about art classes—she went to the High School for Visual Arts. I didn't get any lessons until I enrolled at Cooper Union."

I try to think of what else I can say, "We went ice skating together a couple times, too. There used to be a lot more indoor rinks around the city."

Faith couldn't have looked happier, as though ice-skating rinks were deeply significant. Her head bobs when she says, "We just taped a story for the morning show about ice skating rinks making a comeback. I skate myself. And while I'm not a practicing artist, I do work in a visual medium."

I feel the urge to say something withering back. I don't know why. She is sweet. After Faith rattles off a little more about herself, I blurt out, "My son went to Princeton."

"That's wonderful! You didn't mention him on the phone. So, I have a brother? I mean a half-brother?"

I make myself shrug. I wonder. She is completely natural. She is the human equivalent of a dog that just wants to fetch or a kitten that just wants petting. Well, maybe a kitten with a backbone of steel that carried her through three years of complexity with Ophelia and searching to find me. She seems to want nothing other than my engagement.

Faith turns to her job in television. I try to listen but hearing serves me not as well as sight. I go back to noticing our shared coloring. Her voice is like unlike her birth-mother's at the same age, richer, maybe it's the television training; I realize another difference that probably a true father wouldn't go near. Faith is the kind that is courted, not the kind that is seduced.

She asks the medical questions: Cancer? Heart disease? Alzheimer's? Addictions? Life expectancy?

I answer, she listens.

Then she asks about it being Ash Wednesday. I get the impression she cares more about religion or ethnicity than I do. That gives this young woman, who is over two decades younger than me, a certain air of gravity that resettles itself each time she finishes tossing her hair or giving a dimpled smile.

By now Faith is holding up the conversation for both of us, "Ophelia said you have brothers."

I answer, "One nearby in Long Island. He might as well be a world away. Track house, above ground pool, nothing to talk about. But the other who moved near Cleveland— when we do talk, we can finish each other's sentences."

Mentioning Cleveland is like dangling a shoelace in front of a tabby, and Faith is elated. But I don't remember the street address, don't remember the schools my niece and nephew attend, don't remember the exact years I went out to Cleveland myself. So it goes. I find myself fielding pellets about family, not knowing what is important to tell her. No matter what I say she seems to hang on my every word.

Then I find myself caught up in a narrative about my disorienting years in the army. I shared that with my wife years ago, but not my kids. I'd ended up working as an illustrator for "Stars & Stripes" but hated the solitude while welcoming the escape from the hourly rules of the military hierarchy. My job today reminds me of that time. I left teaching in a private school for the city bureaucracy to better support a family. Hate this very bureaucracy but I've found my own fishing hole within it where I work virtually alone with only one staff.

"In an alternate universe somewhere," I joke with Faith, "I am probably running a commune." Before I catch myself, she breaks out laughing and I am relieved. I bled myself free of metaphors long ago in order to better get along. I didn't mean to slip up now.

"Oh, I know! You want to be creative and not deal with the politics, but you also want human company! A commune or art colony—excellent solution!"

I smile down at my plate and say, "Except I also want to afford a New York City apartment. And *not* in the *outer* boroughs."

The urban snobbery isn't lost on her. Faith pulls her hands off the table.

I admit to myself I intended to say something with just that effect. To push her away, to make the world the way it was before the phone call. When she was missing, as though she didn't exist, when the whole affair was simple, sad and *done*.

I do feel more comfortable now.

She tries another tack, "Who knows about me?"

"My wife," and then I stop, but she picks up that there is more.

"Since I called you last month?"

"No, she doesn't know you called. She doesn't know we're here today," I lean back and let out a sigh, "just off to a normal day at the office."

"That's why you wanted to meet during work hours."

"Right," and then I decide to just let it out, "She knew about it, I told her before you were born."

Faith looks at me, waiting. When I say nothing, she leans in and with a faint voice says, "Ophelia mentioned once an abortionist on Riverside Drive."

I feel crazily relieved to correct an item of fact, "You know, we actually went to two abortionists."

"Oh."

"There was another across the Hudson in Fort Lee, New Jersey."

I must sound to her like the world's first abortion geek. I can't read her reaction. Do I seem manipulative? Trying to distract her from the reality of my giving her away by pointing out that I at least didn't have her aborted?

She is familiar. Certainly, I fathered her. But not familiar enough for me to know the right way to proceed. Her being a stranger is silent testimony to my sin. I think that and then go on.

"You know, we went to two abortionists. I'm pro-choice; you're a choice. When I called to cancel the appointment at the abortionist on Riverside Drive, the nurse said she was really happy to hear that."

Faith smiles, "Thank you."

I almost tell her just before we both lift our cloth

napkins from our laps. I lose my nerve and instead wonder out loud at this place: linoleum tabletops with cloth napkins. Distracted by my own indecision I probably stare a moment too long at the tent that the napkin forms next to my placemat.

Then she asks to take pictures and I decide that the right moment to reveal it has passed. She lifts her camera.

I look up, don't smile. I remember the flash and its too bright after-glare in the mirror. Then I take a deep breath. I start to add sugar to my tea and notice that the double-clink of spoon against cup rim give away that my hand is shaking. I stir the sugar to hide the tremble. Finally, I tighten my knuckles to still my hands on the linoleum space between the plate of eggs over easy and the metal molding of the table's edge. I suspect Ophelia hasn't told Faith. I can understand why. I am amazed at myself that it wasn't the first thing to leave my lips.

I have no idea how I feel about this disaster anymore, no idea how Faith will receive it. I'll just blurt it out.

"I...My fiancé, who was not Ophelia, and I wanted to keep you. My now-wife said, 'This is your child. We'll raise the baby.' We wanted to keep you, Faith."

Faith looks stunned.

Ophelia must not have told her.

What's done is done.

Maybe if I raised her, she'd have always been a reminder to *Rémy* of my infidelity. It would be hard for most women to separate that. Ophelia said no anyway. Ophelia said if I wasn't going to marry her, she was going to give it up for adoption.

I am still talking as I worry a soup spoon, "...If I wasn't going to marry her then she didn't want *us* to have the baby. I really didn't have a leg to stand on, no rights."

"How do you know?"

I shift my one sore hip. "That's how it was back then. It's more complicated than that too. I didn't want to let you go but, no, but I didn't even imagine challenging it in court the way some men do today. I did ask Ophelia to let us keep you. I did want to keep you but I didn't want to break my engagement to Rémy—that's my wife—to marry Ophelia, and that was the only way Ophelia would let it happen. I imagine the adoption agency or the courts would have expected me to marry her too. No, I wanted Rémy and chose her over Ophelia."

Faith says nothing.

I lean forward on my folded arms. I work to keep my shoulders and biceps in decent shape but the skin above my undershirt has softened to match my sixty-some years. I realize suddenly I'm quivering all over. Worse, Faith seems to notice too. Her glance travels back and forth from my folded knuckles to my shoulders, measuring the movement in my sleeves. I blurt out, "Are you angry?"

Then her eyes meet mine.

They are kind and guileless. "No, I'm happy to be alive."

I still look away with a flinch.

It is time to get back. I walk her back to Port Authority —she is catching a bus back to her suburb. As we wait at an avenue light, I tell her more about "Stars & Stripes".

Faith tells me she is making plans to fly to England.

She will be taking a cheap red eye alone to meet Ophelia in London.

In spite of myself, I end up walking Faith to the second level of the bus depot. She turns one last time to smile cheerily and wave at me before climbing into the bus. There is no undertone, no accusation in Faith. I almost wish there were. I could fight back. Instead, I am pulled into waving at the opaque glass of the bus windows as it pulls off, reflections of other bus windows sliding in both directions. I don't know another living soul in my position. I've never met another birth-father.

~ 10 ~

FAITH 2022, LONDON & NEW JERSEY

Faith was letting the truth sink in. Ophelia had cast Bill as treacherously abandoning both her and their child. Now the picture was more nuanced, and maybe more painful: Bill only wanted to leave Ophelia and Bill wanted to keep Faith but believed he couldn't.

Even though she was born on the eve of Roe v. Wade when abortion was illegal, her birth-parents visited not one but two abortionists. *Okay.* One was on Riverside Drive in New York City and the other was across the Hudson River in Fort Lee, New Jersey. Then they decided against an abortion although they were both pro-choice. *Okay.* Then Bill and Rémy tell Ophelia they'll raise Faith but Ophelia spitefully says no.

Faith couldn't even decide if *not* being relinquished would have been better or just different. She would have missed her adoptive mother, Carolyn, but she and her children would have escaped the twisted shadow of her adoptive father and his second wife. Faith would have lived with her own flesh and blood. She might also have been no closer to Rémy's extended family than she was now to some of her adoptive extended family, but she could have grown up *with a brother* in the heart of the *New York City*. She wouldn't have been given away and left with that sense of something missing. Right now, she couldn't go there. She couldn't imagine a childhood without Carolyn, her mother, her best friend, a creative spirit and confidante who somehow was hers to have and to hold.

Faith decided to ask Ophelia her version of things when she got home.

Soon Faith grew frustrated. The trans-Atlantic line crackled periodically during their conversation and, more than that, Ophelia was being evasively mysterious. Ophelia was more interested in how Faith learned the truth than in clearing up this piece of Faith's Chapter One. Faith pressed anyway.

Ophelia persisted, "Oh, I don't like to second-guess myself..."

Faith couldn't quite make out the rest of the sentence, so she apologized and asked her birth-mother to repeat it.

After a pause Ophelia blurted out, "It was he who wanted the baby. He said, 'just go ahead and have the baby, I'll call the clinic to cancel.'"

"I'm sorry."

"And that's pretty much the last I ever heard from the

man. I was left alone, he turned his back, society turned its back, and my own mother said 'Don't expect me to raise it.'"

"I'm sorry."

Faith almost ended the call then. She had given Ophelia the opening to tell her more about Faith's Chapter One and instead it turned into a round of firing blame at everyone else. Faith didn't doubt any of it. Bill probably did say to just go ahead and have the baby without giving it the weight of what Ophelia was about to go through alone. Ophelia's mother, having just finished raising three children, may well have wanted her Cornell-educated daughter to take responsibility. She may indeed have said, "Don't expect me to raise it." But there was no self-reflection from Ophelia. Faith slowly asked, "Is it true that Bill wanted to keep me and you said 'no'?"

Long silence. Then, "Can you imagine what it was like being on the wrong side of society? Can you imagine what it would have felt like seeing him with her *and* you? I wouldn't have that! *I* told *him* that he could stuff it and I was placing it for adoption!"

Ophelia referring to her as "it" instead of a living person with a name and feelings, Faith was taking this in. She heard Ophelia's pain, too, but also the lack of contriteness, remorse.

"And the agency, they didn't teach us we could rebel! They didn't teach us there was any other way. The only counseling I got came at the end when I was told not to date this sort of boy again."

"Then it's true he offered to raise me." Faith didn't

want to keep saying "I'm sorry" anymore. Ophelia hadn't said it for giving Faith away, for delaying their reunion three years, or for denying Bill the chance to raise her. Faith asked a new question, "But after that no one considered anything other than birth?"

"Oh, I suppose you could put it that way, yes."

"Thank you," Faith said.

Ending on a positive note. It was what she would say at the close of an interview for the TV show, more to signal the crew that the conversation was complete. She said it now out of habit, her numbness replacing any real gratitude.

~ 11 ~

BILL 2022, NEW YORK CITY

I avoid Rémy that evening and withdraw to read on our bed next to my bedside lamp in our dark room. I can hear her puttering in the kitchen. Within five minutes I cast aside any pretense of reading and rest my arm over my closed eyes. I lie like that, very still on the bed, remembering a mood from my early adolescence that returns now like a tide.

I discovered a dark, second world then when I was a teenager. The land of when the world was quiet. Lights and flickering TV screens no longer show through windows of the homes around the neighborhood. It was too late for my parents to be awake and see me come home tipsy. Sometimes I'd catch one of the late-night shows, sit with a bag of chips and soda. Sometimes I'd kick my sneakers off, flop down on the family room sofa, stare at the Star-Spangled Banner, then watch the fizzing snow on the screen after the station went off the air.

There was comfort in falling asleep like that out in the

den. Maybe it was the TV light. Maybe it was being in a shared space, same room as where the Christmas tree was decorated, or where the Easter baskets would wait. Yeah, that was it. All that without having to actually speak to my parents. Without having to speak to my parents, I could then go up to my room late and alone with my roiling thoughts.

My parents have long since passed, never knowing they were her grandparents. I inherited the ornaments dusted with Christmases past. But the space of this apartment is mine and there is no need anymore to shut myself in my room like a teenager. Falling asleep on the couch has lost its ability to give me memories of the days when my parents were perfect. That, and I no longer need it to keep their probing questions for daylight.

Now this girl – woman, mother of three – appears in my life. As intrusive, as familiar in smell as my parents, and the same boundless curiosity for my doings and private thoughts. How ironic, what a laugh, this familiarity but this time it is me who is the parent.

* * *

Years ago, when I was known as Willie I preferred the escape of closing doors. Standing with my back to one, shut. If I thought about it, I would have called it the release of silence.

Its opposite happened one afternoon when as a small boy I wandered through the gallery of upstairs rooms at my grandparents' rambling home in the Ozarks. Before he came north, Pa was one of half a dozen children with five living to adulthood. Some rooms are like my friends' homes with doors opening from hallways. But then there are rooms adjoined by two-doored bathrooms and I get to lurk from room to room without bobbing my head out into the main hall where others would see me as they passed. Fear rose in me as I realize the infinite connections. Rooms began to repeat themselves. There were a few rooms that could only be reached through a single entryway from another room. With the gift of years, I could choose *how* to look back and remember them. They were as ordinary as city railroad flats or as ominous as secret chambers.

My grandfather's dressing room was the latter.

I didn't discover it on my early forays. I was content to play in my grandmother's room, found excuses to end my perambulations there. Plush light rug. High fourposter holding the chalk pale colors of a quilt sewn in what she taught me was the tumbling block pattern. A silver tray on a dressing table rested just above eye level, holding her perfume bottles, mesh bulbs to spray or prism stoppers to dab. My grandmother would warn me away gently from either kind by explaining, "They're for girls, and they'll sting your eyes."

Maybe that was the first gentle nudge I felt toward toughening, being a man, and learning when to turn away; I would learn that later but as Willie I was still a sensitive androgenous child with an artist's sensibility.

On either side of the tray were the cut glass bases of empty kerosene lamps. The wicks of their fluted crystal sheaths had each been replaced with narrow sockets and light bulbs. The kerosene basins hung with crystals, trinkets of chandeliers.

When the curtains of the windows on either side of her vanity were parted and the sun poured above the sash just so—light refracted and accordioned brighter off the already clean corners and white furniture legs of the room. I would call grandmother in to see the dancing light. She would pad in almost immediately, bringing with her a hint of lavender sachet.

But down at the far end of a foyer leading from the corner of her room—my grandparents slept separately—was the master bedroom. My grandmother called hers the boudoir, a light sound that matched the crystal. The cavernous room at the end of the narrow hall was called grandfather's bed chamber.

It had the same plush carpet. They had set grandmother's second dressing table there in a corner under one of two high windows. She liked it for the morning light. The dresser held the lipsticks my sisters liked to discover and scoop out of its delicate black wood drawers.

The rest of the room was heavy. A large sleigh bed dominated. Grandfather and grandmother would read together at night until she heard his breathing change. Then she would swing her feet, ankles together, down toward the floor, pointing her toes into her slippers. Grandmother would switch off the lamps around the room, step into the passage to her own room that passed the guest room where Willie slept, and then close the door behind her.

One night, as a very small boy, I woke in the guest room as a great new rumbling rose around me. My door was open.

I measured the distance in the dark from the blanket's edge to the doorframe, then from the doorframe in an arc to my grandmother's room. I took it, elbows and shoulders scrambling against her closed door. She came and opened the door, pausing only to tuck in her chin and laugh before she hoisted me up onto the bed, my legs still scrambling, making circles. She pressed her warm nose against my hair.

"It's just grandpa's snoring."

Still, it was as good a reason as any to sink into the flannel sleeves that smelled like laundry soap. To fall asleep in my grandmother's arms, rocked, held in the boudoir.

The next day I was determined to reinvestigate that bed chamber. I touched the sleigh bed when I walked in. That and the dressing table were my poles and antipoles. Now I pivoted away from their axis and noted the tall ebony chest. Three deep drawers at the bottom, big enough to hold a child like me, even swallow me up in a curled shadow.

Then there were two narrower drawers and the top tier was divided into a pair of book-sized drawers, left and right. The drawer handles were hung in the center of the face of each of the higher drawers. They were ornate at the top like cemetery markers. Curled snakes and fiddleheads of symmetry, they clasped a curlicue handle at each end. Each of the six larger drawers were affixed with an identical handle on their left and right planes. With recent arithmetical wisdom I grasped there were a dozen.

To the right of the towering chest was a door handle, simple, round, with all the promises of a shut door behind it. It stuck a little when I pulled on the knob. What I found once I stepped inside was wonderful even though it was cloaked in darkness. On my left side I touched a long swath of wool that reminded me of the Persian rug in the living room or riding on Grandfather's shoulders; it must be Grandfather's suits. The grownup aroma of cedar stirred from the floorboards as I turned slowly. I caught the sharp odor of men's shoe polish.

There was a cool, metallic trace in the air. I felt a string of pewter beads brush my cheek. When I pulled, the strand turned on the light bulb in its white ceramic collar. Unshielded light made everything step forward at once. My mind took in the inventory. Narrow built-in shelves that climbed above my head to the ceiling. A column of Grandfather's polished shoes. I saw the wing tips. The bottom shelf near my knees held a pair of wooden shoe molds.

Stacked in a neat row on the floor next to me I recognized boxes sealed with a bootblack's kind of origami: the side of each flap tucked under the corner of the flap to its left. This was back before everyone starting using box tape. A row of these cardboard buds, each sealed clockwise, waited. I bent to open one when something brushed my cheek. Cloth, but thick, firm. I looked up.

There was a glare a little to my right that drew my

eye: a mirror. Its joints curved like cupped palms. Within the curved wood frame of a looking glass, the lightbulb, the tarnished gray chain, the woolen suits all hung. The mirror probably reached down to my grandfather's knees with a wide low pair of drawers running below it making a bench. One of Grandmother's doilies lay across the perch. It was low enough that I could still see most of my reflection.

The next thing I noticed was the best. Hanging like Christmas garlands, or the ducks I saw once in the window of a Chinatown shop, were the only brightnesses my grandfather allowed himself. Silk neckties. I stood for a moment, chin jutting up, almost a position of reverence. To be able to reach those one day. To be able to tie those one day. For the first time, the promise of an older self was imaginable.

It was when I backed out of the closet and turned that I saw the looking glass across the room. I walked over to it. It had three panels, the left and right ones swung on their hinges when I gave them a pat. When I stepped forward and folded them in on myself, now I stood at the triangular heart of an intimate funhouse that showed me, cheeks, nose, elbows, and feet from various angles. Once I stepped away, mirror reflected mirror reflected mirror, each with a small child I could see but not touch through the accordions of looking glass rectangles. I didn't like this illusion of a child trapped in frames, back and back and back. I understood the magic trick behind it at the same time that a light cloak of foreboding settled on me.

Where the neckties back hanging in the closet gave

me a vision of possibility, this looking glass, enfolding me in its panels, warned of intractability, of inextricability. I realized I was holding my breath.

I puffed out my lips, pushed open one of the mirrors. Once stepping out, I closed it silently behind me. I felt relieved. Either all the trapped children were freed now, I imagined, or I would not see their confinement.

All these years later, it is the three-paneled looking glass and not the colorful ties of a future possibility that load in my mind's eye. It doesn't matter to me that I sired her, that the trapped child is my own. I don't want to revisit Faith. What is done is done.

It is true. I started to write about the lesson of the folding mirror from that long ago afternoon in the bed chamber. The metaphor that by simply turning our back and folding back a hinged mirror we can make the reflections disappear, we can silence reverberations. The letter is supposed to send Faith a firm message to move forward and forget our encounter, but in spite of my clear purpose, the act of writing veers me in a completely different direction.

I write it longhand because my thoughts flow more freely that way and then type a back-up copy into the computer. I surprise myself by what I write. Rambled is the better word. Finally, I touch a point that shifts everything, like a funhouse mirror and new thoughts come spilling out.

* * *

The next evening, I log out of the computer-assisted design software my son Kieran set up for me and I decide I should give him a call. This young man—five years younger than my birth-daughter—is probably the closest I have to a confidante. I'll call him up, buy him a scotch, tell him something. Writing the letter last night makes me ready. I don't have a plan really; I'll see what comes out.

I tell Kieran over a double malt—at a bar midway between our respective apartments—that I have an older daughter, Faith. About the affair but choosing his Mom, in the end.

Kieran asks me what Faith's like.

I tell him about her working on the television morning show and writing on spec for magazines just like he's making his way as a reporter in the New York City tech press. I tell him she has kids, but that she's fairly silent about her husband and adoptive father and I didn't pry. She speaks happily though about her adoptive mother, an artist. That's probably why the adoption agency placed Faith with them, the art connection between Carolyn Givvers, Ophelia, and me.

Kieran listens, nods, then surprises me by asking, "Why'd you pick Ash Wednesday?"

"Really, it was as soon as I could see her."

"You said you went in the church...."

"No, I went by it. It was on the way." Actually, I did go

in. It was Saint Patrick's Cathedral and I told myself it was like attending a happening. I even joined the line, once I saw it was moving, to receive the sacrament. Feeling the priest mark the cross on my forehead reminded me of catechism. It might have been that long since I'd visited a church.

"Would you have done it if they hadn't named her 'Faith'?"

We both chuckle.

It isn't an answer but my son stops asking me questions. I don't tell Kieran more.

Certainly not the decision his mother and I made to keep Faith and then the powerlessness to make good on that decision. I have enough self-honesty to admit I'm doing it for my own benefit, not his. Then I find myself on the proverbial slippery slope and my stomach feels like it's lined with lead. I know as a parent and as a former teacher that what I'm about to do will put an unfair burden on Kieran.

I ask Kieran to keep this just between us, not to tell his mother I've found Faith.

My son and I finish our drinks and I have another thought, a fleeting memory really.

This I keep to myself as well; I am remembering that requirement of so many reading lists, *The Scarlet Letter*, and what it says in the epilogue. Hester Prynne continues to wear the scarlet letter "A" for adultery, her crime, but she sets up as a seamstress living at the end of a road outside the village. The very townsmen who once ostracized her now seek her out as a skilled embroiderer, ostensibly. But more as the ideal person to confide in. Her own banishment means their secrets will be less likely to be shared, and her own sin means she will be less likely to judge, they calculate. Hester Prynne earns and honors the trust of her customers. Her business flourishes.

Still, she is never welcomed back fully into communal life. That thought makes me feel safe. The things I've told Faith, about work, about myself, are not the kind of confidences I share easily. Faith's isolation from my family, well *her* family too in a sense, serves me well.

* * *

I get another call from Faith. I am sitting in my solitary office and actually look forward to it this time. She reminds me she's flying to Europe to see Ophelia. I don't understand that lost soul who calls Faith and then doesn't come here to visit her. Or maybe I do. Faith says she's just checking in with me before the trip. No, I don't have any message for Ophelia. Well, maybe: hope she's well. There's something else on my mind so I ask to switch topics.

This time I tell Faith that being a graphic designer is only one of my careers. It is true that I started out as a graphic designer like Ophelia. I remember aloud that Ophelia would come up and wait at my desk in the design department of CBS Records where I worked. Eventually I migrated away from the arts to a second career. At the breakfast I told Faith it was a city agency, true as far as that went. I should tell her the truth now. I begin the recitation of my early career...

"What do you do now?" Faith asked.

"I'm the Director of Fiscal Services for Special Needs Adoptions and Foster Care in New York."

"*Wow.*"

"Oh? Why 'wow'?" I say, but I feel a little pleased that it impresses her.

"I guess the relinquishment really had an impact on you." Pow. She must really be trying to sock it to me.

I never saw the connection. "Hmm. I never thought of that before."

I hear muffled laughter on the other end, as though Faith finds my response amusing.

"I'm laughing because we'll never find better testimony than yours, Bill, for the Birth-Fathers' Club case. It'll be a landmark for the adoption and donor-conception heritage equality movement. You, as Director of Fiscal Services for Special Needs Adoptions....Oh, I didn't tell you this yet either: my network is producing a documentary about it. It's really a long slog. There was a test case, delays because of COVID-19, several rounds in the appellate courts, and even the possibility that the U.S. Supreme Court will hear it eventually. This is perfect. You know, Tony of the Tony Silvio Project and Darryl McDaniels of RunDMC have testified for heritage equality. Maybe it's not too late to get you on the witness list to testify...."

Inside something tightens. I keep my answers non-committal, loose. I want to be a decent person but with each question...Any message for Ophelia? Will I testify publicly as a birth-father? Do I want to be captured on tape as a birth-father? ...I feel a wall pushing toward me.

* * *

It's a few weeks later and I know Faith is back from her first visit with my former lover. That was ten days ago and I've been expecting another call from her. She does call, bubbling with brio. She points out it is Holy Week and the week of a fundraiser for the Adoption Triad Circle she belongs to. They are using the story of Passover for an event that focuses on the relinquishment, search, and re-union aspects of the ancient parable. She says something on the other end about "The earth is warming enough to share daffodils and crocuses with us all."

Faith is telling more. How England unsealed its adoption records for adoptees long ago in the mid-seventies. She starts out gushing news from her visit but I know the reluctance of my responses will eventually slow her down. After a few more minutes they do and she sums up the stay as being, "in what remains a stranger's apartment. It was filled with light and artwork and love but also artfully unanswered questions." With that Faith falls silent.

I cringe at her cheerily acknowledged disappointment and therefore, I am sure, the implied burden on me. Faith is counting on me to provide whatever her birth-mother doesn't. Not only will she want me to be her white knight testifying with the Birth-Fathers' Club, she'll especially want to infiltrate my family. I want to embrace her and be that white knight, just as much as I want to make this go away like the echo of mirrors I remembered the night we first spoke. I don't know how this will end, but I plunge in.

"I wrote you a long letter, eight pages."

Faith is silent. She is waiting for me to say more. In the silence feelings seep in to make me thoroughly confused and bereft. Confused, not courageous. Bereft, not brave. All of it is worthless to say to her, I imagine, because I have no words to explain why I didn't fight for her then. Instead of the child exploring my grandfather's closets, I feel like the boy shaking pepper into a soapy bath. I did that once, taken a pepper mill from the pantry even though I wasn't supposed to get into the pantry. When I was caught all my bravado crumbled and I got sent early to bed. But I learned something: the pepper drove the soap away, drove it clear away. Now, on the phone with Faith, I wait, my heart pounding.

Then I blurt it out, "But I tore the letter up. It was all bullshit." It's too late to catch myself. The conversation fades.

I know the cruelty of *I tore the letter up. It was all bullshit* must have stung. Yet—I feel relief at having pushed her away, clear away. Hah, I put a poison pill in this reunion. I chuckle with more than a little self-loathing.

Faith doesn't answer.

I don't stop there, although I'm not exactly sure what my point is. I continue by bringing up again my two brothers I told her about during our meeting at the diner.

I confess I don't know what family ties come down to: the brother in Long Island I have nothing in common with, never see, never miss, brothers only because we have parents in common. Then my thoughts take a pendulum swing and I mention speaking the other night with my brother way out in Cleveland. Whenever we talk, we pick up like old times.

Faith eagerly reminds me that I'd told her my brother and I finish each other's sentences....

~ 12 ~

FAITH 2022, NEW JERSEY

....Faith still heard Bill's voice over the receiver but she was more interested in the hope that was growing in her heart. He was still talking after all, telling her about a brother who mattered to him, and he hadn't hung up even though he tried claiming the letter didn't mean anything to him.

He said that he, Bill, really should tell someone about having found her.

That was a strange thing to say. "Huh?"

"I should tell someone I found you. I haven't told Rémy about you this time."

Faith didn't point out that it was *she* who had found *him.*

Maybe it was a sign he had always been worried about her, some kind of Freudian slip that he had been waiting to find her at some level.

Bill was still talking, now about his son having moved. He rattled off the new address seemingly unintentionally.

Faith copied it down.

Faith was stunned for a moment or two after she disconnected the call. Then she moved to a box of old books in the back of her closet and dragged it out. Her feelings were beginning to crystalize into thoughts as she dug through a double pile of hardcovers and softcovers, lifting books onto the bedroom floor in front of her.

She'd collected dozens of adoption memoirs like these in the years she waited for Ophelia. She had a draft of excerpts and a book agent trying to pitch the idea of an anthology of adoption in fiction and non-fiction. She stretched a rubber band over her fingers and then cupped them over a pile of notecards, her notes for the same manuscript. Tony Silvio's and Betty Jean Lifton's memoirs were somewhere in these stacks too.

Not sure why but, she made a quick call to BJ who greeted her warmly. BJ listened patiently as Faith jabbed at what Bill's letter might have contained.

BJ had a suggestion.

Faith listened and after the call decided to write down in a spiral notebook her thoughts. As a rule, Faith avoided journaling because it felt too much like her job: turning real life into packaged stories. At work, everyone in the writers' room teased Iwami-san, a cameramen, because his only hobby outside of work was taking still photographs: "Get some variety, dude." But after this conversation with BJ, Faith decided to give it a try.

BJ offers to be an intermediary and speak to Bill for me as a kind of relationship broker. I demur, deciding Bill's and my dance is meant for two not three. She also offers to be my therapist. My head knows she's well-intentioned but my heart retreats from what feels like two offers that could lead to unequal power relationships. I don't need that right now.

I'm already crawling out from those years of waiting for Ophelia. Or waiting for laws to change. I'm open to seeing a therapist when it makes sense. Right now, it's my quest and I have questions not issues.

As I write this here in my journal, I realize I don't believe I'm entitled to a relationship with Bill. But Bill, like any birth-father, owes his child at least a meeting. I realized after I hung up the phone that this is what I believe in my heart of hearts. That and I don't feel like hounding him the way I'd hound a good lead for a news story. It's like those memes say: the disrespect is closure enough.

Maybe it really was just "bullshit" to him.

This whole reunion feels like a dance. Not those self-help books, Dance of this, Dance of that, but like walking into a real dance where you get a sense of someone by how they move. I don't pursue someone who seems uninterested or not interested enough. I don't want to do that to myself at a club or in this birth-family reunion. To keep going with the dancefloor metaphor, sometimes whether you put your drinks up and get on the floor depends on what music is playing in your life too. When someone asked me why I waited three years before I flew to see Ophelia, I told them the answer was my small children. The constancy of their needs and my love for them was the music that was playing in my life then (and ever since).

The timing of Ophelia's call was on Ophelia's timetable not mine. That, and I wasn't going to chase someone who seemed to vacation with apparent frequency and casually break her promises to visit. The third time she talked about flying in for my birthday was the last. She cancelled again, saying she'd lucked into getting a free ticket to see Mother Meera in Germany, some kind of mystic who would hug strangers in a way that made them feel maternal love and who claimed to be an avatar of the Divine Mother.

Going to gaze in Mother Meera's eyes was an experience of spiritual growth, Ophelia informed me.

I suggested, half amused, half stunned, that Ophelia keeping her word to her only child might be an experience of spiritual growth.

Looking into her daughter's and grandchildren's eyes instead of a guru's might be the real growth.

The woman who wrote letters to my adoption agency, who attended a natural mother support group in London for years, went through with the trip to Mother Meera and cancelled the plans to see us.

The grandchildren were done with her. It would be many years before I was anything but numb. We became hardened to Ophelia. It was tragic really. I found self-protective tricks: I noticed when our connection was by phone she was in touch more often, less if I wrote her a letter. She could wait months before acknowledging a letter, I imagined her re-reading rather than replying, so I stopped writing to her.

It was me who flew to see her first, girding myself with backup itinerary, telling myself it would solve the mystery once and for all – what mystery I wasn't sure. I met my birth-father only a few weeks before I met Ophelia – so I could forget birth-parents once and for all, but after. Then I let myself create a scrapbook of our meetings.

I am attached to her, still recognize and like her smell. I am not sure the open adoption she now says she wishes we had would have been better for me. Knowing that she gave me a name, what we adoptees commonly call a birth-name, would have been good for me.

Knowing much sooner what my Grandpa Eddy eventually told me when I was a late teen would have been good for me too. The family patriarch who founded a local chain of hardware stores, Channel Home Centers, was also adopted into the Givvers clan.

Knowing my heritage from my father would have been better for me than growing acclimated to an absence of heritage because of the taboo around being Indigenous.

For me, with Bill, a sense of wanting to let things play out naturally, not force a relationship, is true. He has my number. He has my email. After talking to me that way, the ball is in his court. If his way of being a birth-father in the world is to work for the city of New York, writing checks every day to foster parents and adoptive parents, then that's his right.

I don't have to like that he fails on the personal level as my birth-father and as a grandfather to my kids.

I don't have to like that he didn't fight more for me after Ophelia pushed back and said she would not let him and his wife raise me.

I don't have to like that he could have done so much more with this reunion.

When I'm ready, on my time and not Ophelia's or Bill's, I will contact my brother Kieran. I had so bought into the children's book, The Chosen Baby, *that most adoptees of a certain age grew up with that I disassociated myself from loss and from the societal shame that invited secrecy and sealed records.*

The Chosen Baby, *where we were more special than others, was a sharp contrast to the* Leave It to Beaver *episode that was my husband's childhood primer for how to react to adoption. There, being adopted was being unchosen, less than, and a shameful state. Despite my adoptive parents' best efforts, I soaked in that message too.*

Fast forward to when I'm a teen. I remember reading Nathaniel Hawthorne's The Scarlet Letter *and writing a book report for English. Pearl was the teenage daughter and Mr. Dimmesdale was her father. Somehow, I didn't associate it with me. I didn't associate that scarlet letter with some people's responses to adoption and donor conception to this day.*

Now I do. I get that I was never really the chosen baby. I wasn't even un-chosen. I was a bit player.

Now I do the choosing and I choose love. Here it is. The passage where Pearl meets her birth-father, but only once, like me.

> As Pearl kissed Mr. Dimmesdale's lips, a great spell was broken....as her tears fell on her father's cheeks, they were the pledge that she would grow up amid human joy and sorrow, nor forever do battle with the world, but be a woman in it....

I will let go of the family who choose fear and cutoff instead of compassion. I have to. I choose love and possibility, but oh, this is hard.

~ 13 ~

BILL 2023, NEW YORK CITY

A few months later I get a call from Kieran telling me Faith has looked him up. Maybe this is how it is going to play out.

"Are you surprised Dad?"

"No, meet her. It would be fine if you two meet."

She'll be calling me again next.

Kieran reports back that they met after work at the Malibu Diner. I like that one, but it is a younger crowd, down in Chelsea not too far from the Flatiron on 23rd Street.

For a few weeks I ask and Kieran tells me that he and Faith are emailing. Faith and Kieran even talk about his maybe catching a train out to visit. I don't ask more and Kieran senses that I don't want to talk about it.

Over the next few months, I don't hear anything more of Faith, either directly from her or from Kieran. I live with a smooth undercurrent of knowing she's turned out okay. I wonder occasionally if I will ever hear from her again. I am a little relieved that I haven't so far.

I wonder if I should take it back—it isn't bullshit after all. I decide I will leave the ball in Faith's court. If she ever reaches out again, I will apologize. If she asks what I wrote, I will tell her. Otherwise, I tell myself, maybe a little self-servingly, my silence will leave her in peace.

Part 4

FAITH
"'What's the new normal after a reunion?' Now after a couple years in? It's relationships with some family members and not with others. I found people I like knowing. I have ancestors like everyone else. That grounds me. Going on the quest changed me by making me more centered."

SOLOMON
"The new normal is I'm one of my daughter's biggest fans. Susan said she learned from going back to her birth-country that some losses are for keeps. That's true. For me, I will never have what her adoptive parents have. But I am happy for every visit, every phone call."

SUSAN
"'What's the new normal after a reunion?' Having one more person to love. Learning to see redemption in absurdity. Faith and I were just talking about that."

~ 14 ~

SUSAN 2023, NEW YORK CITY

One Thursday a few weeks later, Susan hosted the opening of "Changelings in Folk Art and Legend" at the Argot. It was invitation-only and she wore an Issake print with embroidered panels. She fielded two interviews with the press, the last one in the courtyard between two potted arrangements of *suzuki* and *sasa* grasses a dear friend on the Board of Trustees provided just for this exhibit.

When the second interview was done and one of the camera crew was removing the mic clip from her neckline, Susan was surprised to hear the next question, off-air. It came from the field producer named Anita who had just finished interviewing her. Anita stepped back toward Susan and spoke over the sound of clicks and snaps as the crew packed up.

Anita had been intelligent but a little on the aggressive side for an arts interview. She tapped her fingertips to her collarbone as though touching a pendant. Her sandy colored lashes were mascaraed and for that Susan gave her credit, but her lips were chapped and her straight, light hair was kept in an unflattering cut. Strange for someone working in a visual medium.

Anita must have some other spark, reasoned Susan, to hold her own in the tough field of reporting the New York arts scene. Anita cleared her throat, apparently trying to sound nonchalant, "I have a changeling story of my own."

That caught Susan's attention. She looked forward to having a more human connection than had just happened during the interview itself.

Anita tilted her head before saying, "I got contacted recently by a true 'changeling'."

Then she gave a dry little laugh.

"What do you mean?" Susan asked.

"You wouldn't believe what she did.

"What? Who?" Susan asked pleasantly.

"She walked right up to me at a media event. She's from back East, too, but we were both there with the rest of our LA offices. She's on the content side. She walks right up, holds out her hand, and introduces herself as my 'half-sister'."

Susan searched Anita's face to try and understand feelings that already promised to be so different from her own. Susan wanted to at least start there. Anita seemed to expect Susan to share her indignation. Like sticking her toe in a swirling current, Susan tried out, "I guess it was a bit of a surprise. A sister you never knew about. And meeting her in a work context. You must have been blown away."

Anita seemed satisfied and nodded, "Right there. At this big event."

"Was this in front of other people?"

"No, she waited until I was standing off on my own."

"You felt ambushed anyway?"

"Of course."

"You kind of wish she had reached out privately first. She could have; she obviously knew who you were," offered Susan.

"She said she'd written to me first, earlier. She'd sent a handwritten envelope to my office in the New York City headquarters. It was certified mail so she could confirm its delivery whether I chose to acknowledge it or not. The mailroom signed for it, but I don't open envelopes if I don't recognize the sender. You know," said Anita.

Susan nodded as if she did.

Susan wanted to hear the rest of the story so she said nothing about what a missed opportunity she felt that had been. She was curious, but not in the way Anita must have imagined; Susan wanted to know why anyone would not *welcome* a sister.

Anita went on with effort, "She met my dad, twice it seems. She'd come from whatever bridge or tunnel and they'd meet..." She swallowed and then shrugged.

Susan wasn't sure how to take the dated, lazy, "bridge or tunnel" dig at the two-dozen million people of the tri-state area who lived outside the island of Manhattan. She focused on her next question.

"So, she met your father. He never told you?" asked Susan.

"They were only brief visits," added Anita.

Susan tread carefully. "Sure. But what I mean is he didn't tell you he had another daughter; you had a sister he was meeting in the city? What happened exactly?"

"First of all, she was almost five years older than me. But it was really because of—get this – she refused to take a DNA test."

"Of course. She said her birth-mother had given her conflicting information on the birth-father. She actually contacted other men with the same name. But they said 'no'. My father was the only one to say 'yes,' so obviously she had some doubt," Anita said.

Susan asked, "Is it a common name? That would explain why she had to contact more than one person. I wonder what it was like for her to make cold calls looking for her own birth-father."

"Well, I don't wonder."

This hard-bitten producer hadn't given Susan an opening for human warmth. Anita must still be in shock. Susan decided to keep her own story, or that of dozens of other such sisters she knew, to herself. She also noted silently that they had reversed roles, it was she who was now gently interviewing Anita, the producer, "But your father agreed to meet her again after the first visit. It sounds like they both believed it was a match. Does she look like you?"

"Brown eyes, same height. It could be anybody. She refused to take a DNA test."

"She may have felt insulted. Especially since your father recognized her."

"She should have understood my concern."

"Oh, is there an inheritance involved? Do you think she might be scamming you?"

"No, she never asked about it. She's married with kids, all set up it seems. She asked about other things. I just couldn't give her what she needed."

"Too personal?"

"No, it's just she didn't understand that she was looking for the man who fathered a baby before he and my mother married. She didn't understand that I knew him as a father and she didn't."

"Hmm. What kind of questions did she ask?"

"All sorts. What kind of foods did my dad like? Did he like to read? Did he have hobbies? Was he outgoing? My father and I were so close that I didn't think of him that way. This person was looking for a different man."

"'What kinds of food did your father like?'"

"Okay, well, I really only started to think about him that way in his last year, when he was ill. Before then we were so close."

It sounded, to Susan, like Anita wasn't ready to admit how little she knew her beloved father, that this sister possibly wanted to know him in ways she'd never reached.

Could this be, Susan wondered with amazement, a new bloom on the twisted branch of sibling rivalry?

Susan spoke next with hesitation.

"So maybe this stranger came in seeing him as a

separate person, asking questions right up front that you had only recently begun to ask."

Anita shook her head, looking confused.

"No, what killed me was that my brother knew. He'd already known about her for a year and didn't tell me."

"A lot of secret keeping."

"He claims that I'm having problems with her because now I'm not the only daughter. But get this..."

Susan waited as Anita shifted a strap on her shoulder.

"My brother thought our father must have been seduced. He couldn't picture him as a college student choosing to have, ah, a serious relationship with anyone before Mom. For me, it's just I can't help that woman, like I explained to you."

Susan paused and took in this daughter who was realizing that the father she adored was a cipher to her. *I wonder what on earth she means by "help" here.* Susan tested out another idea.

"It is so unfair to be the last one to know."

The woman looked perplexed.

This might not be the time for her to welcome a sister but I can at least offer her something for when that time ever arrives.

"Anita, listen, I may have some information for you around processing reunions. What's your number?"

Anita's moment of openness closed and she said, "You can reach me through the network switchboard."

Anita turned back to her crew who were packed up now.

~ 15 ~

FAITH 2023, NEW JERSEY

"Oh, Susan, you'll never believe what my birthmum is doing now. Ophelia was asked to make a sculpture for an anniversary exhibit of the opening of British adoption records back in the nineteen seventies," Faith said. She and Susan were walking on a boardwalk that threaded through the ponds and marshes of a local a woodland near Susan's home. They caught up over the soundtrack of birdsongs and the surprises of ducklings and a blue heron on the hunt.

"Who asked her?" asked Susan.

"The Royal Academy something-or-other where she's had exhibits before."

"I thought Ophelia was a painter and printmaker. So, she's doing sculptures now? What is it?"

"She is crafting a geodesic dome, she says, meaning a semi-circular shape like an igloo or a yurt, but made out of triangles: light but strong," said Faith.

"I've seen the one at Montreal from the old World's

Fair. Buckminster Fuller designed the concept. You told me once you interviewed him as a kid. Is that why she picked triangles and a geodesic dome?"

"No, I don't think so. Ophelia and I don't talk much about things I did in the past. She won't let me talk much about her past. She insists she just wants to live in the present, 'not second-guess' herself, so this geodesic dome is a switch for her. She's actually using them to hint at our shared past, her way. Triangles are the heart of the structure and Ophelia says they represent each side of the 'adoption triangle' or 'donor triangle'."

Susan laughed, "I get it! For each side of the 'adoption triangle': adoptees, adoptive parents, and first or birth-parents. For the 'donor triangle': donor-conceived people or DCPs, right? And then recipient parents or intentional parents, and missing DNA relatives."

"Yes, but remember this is beloved birthmum. She tells me, 'Faith, love, I've hit on an absolutely brilliant idea!' *She is building the triangles out of test sticks.* Ovulation test sticks. Pregnancy test sticks. And DNA sticks from both paternity tests and genealogy tests," said Faith and let out a teenager-worthy groan.

Susan considered a moment, then said, "She's right. It *is* brilliant. It has a sense of humor. Yet it says something about how profoundly retail science has become part of our private lives. Or new ways we relate to our bodies, to our ancestry, to our descendants. It's perfect for the Royal Academy-whatever. You should be proud of her."

Now that Susan said that, Faith realized she could indeed be proud of Ophelia. She didn't really want to make fun of her birth-mother. She guessed she did it to pre-empt anyone else doing it. Faith said, "Yes, I am. She's pretty original."

Then Faith decided to share something else with Susan. "Hold on, Ophelia sent me a picture of different artwork she's already completed. As a curator you can appreciate this. It's made of metallic foil wrappers –"

"– They're probably what the test sticks came in –"

"– No doubt. But it looks like a medieval tryptic of Jesus, his recipient father St. Joseph, and the Heavenly –"

"– the Heavenly Father as a male donor?!? I don't think I can breathe! That's hysterical. It's beautiful," and Susan put her hand on Faith's shoulder as she caught her breath.

Faith couldn't help smiling, "The point is Jesus loved both."

"You come from good stock, sweetie."

Search and reunion, Faith had come to realize, was the kind of life event that made its subjects look at their previous memories anew. Sometimes, it made them feel more like the very subject of their own life than they had ever been before, it gave them a room of their own with walls woven by DNA. Their presence, their understanding made them a more deeply-dyed figure to themselves than all the others—siblings, parents, teachers, friends—who until that time had dominated the scroll of their personal tale.

* * *

The matriarchs in the Hebrew Bible were Sarah, Rebecca, Rachel and Leah. Faith's were Ada, Paula, and Carolyn. Mom was Carolyn, of course, and she took many avatars, many forms over the course of the reunion. Not to be confused with Ophelia her birth-mother overseas.

Paula was Faith's paternal grandmother who died in her sixties, a matriarchal force neither formidable nor gentle. She died when Faith was five and it was almost impossible to remember her face, but Faith remembered her table. She remembered the long holiday table where grownups – aunts, uncles, and the grandparents' generation – sat and the sofa nearby where Faith and their cousins bounced or ate.

Ada was Carolyn's Mom and her favorite grandmother whom she called Bamie; her grandfather was Bampie. Faith named her own daughter, Ada, in honor of her. Bamie was one of those people who had times when she read the Bible every day either because she was moved by its poetry and antiquity, or because it was a companion in a battle no little granddaughter could understand. Bamie was the one who gave Faith her own King James Bible and hymnal in a neat, zippered case that Faith still kept. She could still remember the way the faux leather handles felt when she carried it on Sunday morning. She would give it to Ada someday.

She wondered what Bamie and Bampie would have thought about her search and reunion. She drew a blank. They both died when Faith was a college freshman and she couldn't picture ever discussing relinquishment with the warm, affectionate grandparents that seemed so far from that world. There was something else, too, she simply didn't know Ada as an individual despite how much she loved Bamie.

With a sudden epiphany Faith understood Anita, that icy television producer who came to Susan's "Changelings in Folk Art" opening. Anita had told Susan she rejected her own sister because, essentially, it made Anita realize how little she knew their shared father. How disorienting to realize you didn't know well, and had lost the chance to know, someone who was the center of your world. For Anita it was her father who she never knew was also a birth-father. For Faith it was her beloved Bamie.

If Bamie were supportive, still warm and available during her search, Faith would love her even more than she already did, something nearly impossible. If Bamie scolded, used stinging words like "at least you weren't placed in an orphanage", if she otherwise withdrew, Faith would have stumbled down a dark corridor from which their connection would never have been the same.

Growing up, Carolyn was always what Faith and her friends thought of as a tough broad. She had an edge. She worked in fashion long beyond when other women her age had found a man, moved to the suburbs, and voluntarily sacrificed their smarts. But once Carolyn did marry out to the burbs, she set up a small studio in a basement room where she pounded and soldered precious metals into jewelry and melted plexiglass sheets into those pectoral sculptures that Susan had researched. Faith's Mom once described motherhood to Faith as *menial*. In fact, most of her friends had chosen to forego motherhood whether by adoption or birth. Nevertheless she was there as a parent. She was very proud when her influence manifested itself in Faith's knack for all things visual and then when Faith went into television production. Even with her beloved mother, the search and reunion changed something core, at least for a first fitful year.

Faith and Carolyn both were caught by surprise when it turned out Ophelia was a working artist, a printmaker and painter. Like Carolyn, Ophelia had a studio, in a London flat not far from Hampstead Heath. Faith was elated. Carolyn was devastated. Faith wasn't the blank slate the adoption agency had promised and had, in fact, arrived with some inborn artistic talent. She was more than a reflection of Carolyn's artistic glory. Faith felt betrayed by Carolyn's disappointment. It would take years for Faith to see past what she assumed must be her mother's egotism and jealousy to the fear beneath it. Few women, let alone mothers, were welcome on the urban art scene then. Faith came to understand that perhaps her mother feared losing an artistic and personal connection with the daughter she raised, to an artist who had made it, Ophelia.

Now it would be like more fresh salt in those wounds if her mother knew that her birth-father had at least briefly worked as a graphic designer at CBS Records. Faith decided to focus on her television career and her own children. She told herself she just wanted to live her life.

* * *

Then on Father's Day the next year DNA test kit ads were everywhere. They could have renamed Father's Day "paternity test day". *Why Father's Day and not Mother's Day? Had no one caught on that some parents were lying to their donor-conceived kids just as some parents lied a generation earlier to their closed-adoption kids?* Her kids and husband caught the bug and by Christmas Day she found herself unwrapping his- and hers- DNA test kits from Ancestrology. Her husband looked over at her and said, "I hope we don't turn out to be cousins."

"Oh, I think we're done with surprises. Remember I took that 6DegreesOfSeparation DNA test when it was on sale a few years ago? Nothing interesting at all plus a lot of unidentified DNA for what are probably my Indigenous ancestors."

"6DegreesOfSeparation has a database of people several times smaller than the database on Ancestrology, plus more people have signed up in the years since. That's why you didn't find anything."

The days went slowly before Faith got a notice in her Inbox telling her the results were ready. Before she logged on to the site, she texted Susan to come over and together they brushed breakfast's toast crumbs off the kitchen island.

Then Faith pulled her DNA results up on the laptop and

they took two kitchen stools. They clicked to the webpage with her results.

This is too fast, thought Faith. "Look at this page, I have five hundred and thirty-seven potential family members! I've gone from being a genetic orphan to this. Where do I start?"

"First one step, then the next," Susan said and gave Faith's arm a squeeze.

Faith inhaled, "Right. I mean, it looks like there are two layers. See," Faith said and pointed, "First, they give us the option to turn off the 'relative finder' function. This is for relatives as close as second cousins. Someone told me that even though they give you results like 'sixth cousin' these retail kits are really only accurate to fourth cousins. Especially for ethnic groups where there's been a lot of intra-marriage. That makes descendants appear more closely related than they are."

"What are you going to do?" asked Susan.

"Well, first I'm taking a screen capture for the documentary."

"Would you like me to take a video of you opting in too?"

Faith hesitated and Susan read her mind.

"I know, it'll look amateurish but, hey, hashtag #lived-experience. Where should I stand?"

"Okay, sure. Thanks. Here, let me move you," Faith said as she positioned Susan where her device camera could get the widest angle of the Ancestrology screen but still block the kitchen light's glare.

Faith sat back down slightly in front of Susan, clicked, and then a dialogue box appeared.

"What's this? The pop-up is explaining how this 'new' evidence of a close family relationship can be unexpected and even upsetting," Faith clicked through.

A second pop-up appeared on screen.

"Whoa, now here's another warning. Oh, no, Susan, is this really happening?"

"It's happening. We got this, Faith! Go on."

"It's asking me to click 'Yes' or 'Cancel' to confirm whether I *really* want to know who it is. Too much!"

Susan leaned next to Faith and scanned the message, "That can't be normal."

"Right? Hang on, I'll take a screen shot to save this for the documentary too. Okay, here it is:

'You may learn information about yourself that you do not anticipate.

Such information may provoke strong emotion.'"

Then Faith leaned back and looked at Susan, "My palms are getting sweaty."

"Ten jumping jacks?"

"You're nuts. But, okay, it'll help me chill out," said Faith climbing down from her seat. The jumping scared the cat from the room but not Artie, the dog. He watched Paws scamper but didn't move his own belly from the nice cool kitchen floor. When Faith and Susan sat back down at the counter Faith cleared the screensaver, a picture from last summer of Artie and Paws together watching a squirrel.

"Ready now," said Susan. Susan pressed 'VIDEO' on her device.

"Okay, clicking 'Proceed'. What's this? **'You and Melissa Hauben, Close Family up to 1st Cousin, 22% shared DNA: 1,531 cM across 37 segments**." Faith paused, "Then over here, Susan, it says under 'Possible DNA relationships' that ninety-nine percent of the time, people who share this many cMs have the following relationships: Grandparent; Grandchild; Half sibling; Aunt/uncle; and, Niece/nephew' I can't believe this is happening!"

~ 16 ~

BILL 2023, NEW YORK CITY

I know it is long past the time to learn about "social", the Internet, all of it.

Everyone on the art scene has their portfolios up on social media platforms. I know this because more than once I've heard gallery owners on the phone asking for an artist's social media handle to see their portfolio online. I've been gainfully employed all these years with the City, but I've always wanted to be part of an exhibit, always wanted to be invited to be in a show. This might be my way in. It's time to set up my own social media accounts at least. Then I can decide who to follow or friend, heart or like, and re-tweet or share. I search a few platforms to make sure the name I want isn't taken. Got it. I set up @billyardNYC and for my profile image upload – pretty clever, I think – a photograph of billiards!

Something possesses me and I look for "Faith Givvers" and I recognize the face instantly. I don't need to connect to read her posts because it's public. I scan the top thread that has sixty-some Hearts and close to a hundred Comments. As I start to catch on, my stomach knots and my hands grow icy.

Faith Givvers February 23, 2023

THANKS IN ADVANCE FOR ANY HELPING HAND.

I got my results from Ancestrology and am bouncing off walls:

there is one "close family to 1st cousin" who is also an ADOPTEE!!!!! 😳

☺

I have tried every way I know to reach her through that site and elsewhere. No answer yet. Grrrrrrrrrrrrrrrrrrrrrrrrrrrrrrrrrr.☹

How do we tell if we're half siblings (same birth-father) or first cousins (one of my two biological uncles would be her birth-father)?????

We share first and second cousins matches to whom I've also sent messages. 😭😭😭

61 Hearts   96 Comments   1 Share

Faith Givvers CeCe Moore?

CeCe Moore Look at the total cMs.

Faith Givvers CeCe Moore: cMs?

CeCe Moore centimorgans - how many do you share?

Faith Givvers CeCe Moore 1,531 cM across 55 segments

CeCe Moore Congrats, you have a half-sibling (or an aunt/niece/grandmother)!

Faith Givvers Really????❤❤❤

CeCe Moore Yep! That is a second degree relative.

Faith Givvers CeCe Moore - she appears to be ten or so years older than me. As Ancestrology says close family-1st cousin, is it possible that she might also be a 1st cousin with those numbers? My birth-father had/has 2 brothers....

CeCe Moore (First cousin would be third degree.)

Faith Givvers CeCe Moore -just saw this: THANK YOU!!!

CeCe Moore Nope, definitely not a first cousin.

CeCe Moore 100% certainty – check **Blaine T. Bettinger**'s Project 5.0 Tool v4 with relationship probabilities. *[hyperlinked]*

Faith Givvers She's not on Facebook but I will try sending this to her via the Ancestrology site. I hope she is as thrilled as I am!!! YYAAAAAYYYYYYYY!

CeCe Moore I hope so too! How do you know she is an adoptee?

Faith Givvers CeCe, on her Ancestrology description directly under her name she wrote this publicly (I guess she wants to be found, eh?)...

"Valley Stream, Nassau, New York, USA

I was adopted. The only info I have is: Birth-mother, S---- K--------, but she used an alias that sounded Jewish, Marcia Cohen, on my original birth certificate. She denies Hebrew heritage although she went to a Jewish adoption agency, her own mother's name and place of birth are typically Jewish, and I test one-quarter Jewish."

...

Faith Givvers Thanks to **Blaine T. Bettinger** also for the Shared cM Project Tool. And while I'm giving credit where credit is due, I need to name check an old crime fiction author, publisher, and general power behind the throne, **Austin Camacho**, who introduced me to **Jamie Freveletti, David Swinson**, and **S.A. Cosby.** He published short stories of ours in a well-regarded crime fiction anthology. The main character in my short story "Know When to Hold 'Em" finds an older sister through a DNA test...

AC: I remember it!

Faith Givvers: You're on this thread!? It's crazy, isn't it?

AC: This isn't a case that can be explained by life imitating art. Maybe you have a sixth sense. **Faith,** I believe there is a reason we were drawn to writing mysteries.

...

Faith Givvers Uh-uh: she's not answering!!!!

RS Patience ...you have waited your entire life you can wait a short time longer. Hugs you have this. Faith Givvers initial reaction is what does she want from me ... it takes a moment for our families to understand we want nothing but knowledge.

...

SS-F She may not be searchable. If you'd like I can run her name.

Faith Givvers SS-F - I'd like to PM you tomorrow, if that's okay.

SS-F Faith Givvers sure

SS-F I have also found out recently, if you invite a person to a tree, their email shows when you go to who you've invited to your tree. I made a fake tree to use for this purpose.

...

Faith Givvers This morning it occurred to me that she really COULD be an aunt (2nd degree separation just like a half sibling) because my paternal grandparents were young enough to have a "change of life baby" around the time she was born. Could they have decided, despite being married and having raised children, to place their last one for adoption???

TO When you speak with her, the two of you can review your shared matches. This may shed some light rather quickly if you both have matches that the other one doesn't have. This will be helpful if you have close matches on both the maternal and paternal side.

Faith Givvers ❤

SNB Faith Givvers yes that does happen, especially if they hid the pregnancy.

JB This is fantastic and I hope you will keep sharing how this works out!

Faith Givvers Thanks, J.

SN Faith Givvers very exciting. answers are going to move for you now.

...

Faith Givvers I made 15 phone calls this afternoon, wireless and landline, to numbers that *might* belong to my adoptee sister. So far: wrong numbers, no longer in service, or I left a message. The top wireless one listed had a recording I've never encountered before about the caller settings would not allow this call to be completed...? I know you can whitelist chats, and I guess this means you can whitelist cellphone calls...?

JL Faith Givvers, oh man.... I did all of that.... so nerve racking!!! ❤❤❤

JJ Use more than one match and see how they all fit. It's a puzzle

Faith Givvers I realize she was able to build a family tree on Ancestrology with her birth-mother's parents, 2 kids and husband on it who don't match any of mine. That rules out her being an aunt with my bio grand-parents as her parents, probably – she was born in 1955, That leaves only our birth-father as the connection. Bill and I have Native American/Indigenous heritage but she doesn't show any.

JJ Aw, honey, you know already this isn't complete genome sequencing, right? All these test kits just pick some segments to test and the particular segment may or may not have markers for that particular heritage even though that heritage is there.

Faith Givvers No, I didn't know that. So, they test just a few samples, not all our DNA?

...

I scroll back and forth between the typed post and one photo of Melissa that Faith has left in the thread. Not so fast! I check the year Faith says that woman was born. I do some quick genealogical arithmetic. I was still a student. I would have known if my parents had a change of life baby in 1958. Ophelia would have been too young at that point. Why is she ruling out either of my brothers? Let me look at Melissa's picture again.

From the eyes up she does look like me.

From the eyes down...

I take a long moment. Melissa's lips are closed but smiling, a little like... Suzie Kahaly's? The radio was playing "Wake Up, Little Suzie" back then. The chin? Yes. She's older than Suzie was then but, yes.

How could it be? We didn't date that long. We did make love.

I met her parents only once. Rebecca and John? Rebecca looked like she might be Jewish, had some kind of accent that wasn't Gaelic but she claimed to be part Irish like me. If Suzie Kahaly got pregnant, she never told me. Did she break up with me or did I break up with her?

Back to her mother Rebecca. Back in those days I'd say I was Irish to non-family. I told Kieran and Faith about my Cherokee grandmother, the trips south to visit her growing up. We weren't Oklahoma Cherokee; we were Eastern Band.

Here in New York City, we didn't have the term 'urban Indian' and we didn't realize New York had a large Indigenous population. New York may be one of the first cities of the world but it's also the second capital for many small tribes: second largest Puerto Rican and Taino population outside Puerto Rico. Second largest Jewish population after Tel Aviv, Israel. Why not largest Indigenous population outside a rez? But we never knew each other.

No one had written a book yet named after the site of Crazy Horse's killing by the U.S. Army, the site where Crazy Horse's parents came to bury his heart and some of his bones, *Bury My Heart at Wounded Knee*. I had never even heard of an American Indian Movement until the seventy-one-day standoff at Pine Ridge, South Dakota.

Our own people – Cherokee, my mother said but then a cousin insisted grandma was also Choctaw – stayed in the South except for my father. We had cousins in Broken Arrow, Oklahoma, the southern Ozarks in Arkansas and on the other side of the Mississippi River from Memphis to Defeated Creek, Tennessee. Defeated Creek got its name when the Cherokee defeated European marauders. When my father took us back, any visit involved a few stops because the cousins and aunts and uncles were scattered across both states.

Back to Defeated Creek where the leader of the victors went on to become a Cherokee chief for about a decade or so until a White militia ambushed him while he was on a diplomatic mission to Knoxville. They murdered his wife, Betsy, and maimed him. Even though the creek already had a good Cherokee name, 'Defeated Creek' stuck. History belongs to the victors. That kind of thing hung in the air if you were a Native American. Maybe that's why my father left and came north to New York City. Somehow though when he married Ma, he was marrying into a Mohawk Haudenosaunee line transplanted to New York.

I sigh, then chuckle. Ophelia knew all this. The adoption agency knew we were Native American. Kieran even attended Brown University as a Cherokee. Our history, Faith knew none of it. The good or the bad.

Words like the S-word or 'dirty Indian' are too much a part of the culture to not slide into being something else if you can. Irish. All the cops and the politicians here to this day are Irish. The Yards became Irish. Maybe that's why Suzy's Russian-born mother "became" Irish too. We do have some claim on Ma's side. An ancestor with no surname who went by Dinah was said to have had a wilderness husband from Ireland. Later, when she married a Kemp and converted to Christianity, she kept some of her first love in her son's middle name, Murphy. Benjamin Murphy Kemp. Was Murphy, the wilderness husband, a birth-father too?

It could be. I could have two daughters out there, Faith and Melissa, not just my son Kieran. I resume reading Faith's thread with a little fear, a little wonder.

Lorraine D Rooting for a happy outcome!

Faith Givvers Oh, Lorraine, it has been some week. After making all the cold calls to people who *might* be her or know her, sending emails and texts, I decided to try looking for her through sources of images that looked like her in google search results. The one I found tells the story. It is posted directly after this on my wall, the day after this post. (But I know they appear in all different orders in these social media feeds.)

LD Faith Givvers, Hugs.

Then a while later I see....

<<**Image contains**: "Can you show me proof">>
Faith Givvers Don't you hate this?

I write to one of several people on social who have the same name as a 1st cousin on Ancestrology. One woman in her first two replies asks questions I've already answered. Maybe she's in shock. 😵

Then instead of either logging into Ancestrology and checking or admitting that she doesn't have an account and therefore can't be the right person, she feels entitled to demand proof. I politely refuse and flip the script, explaining that unless she can establish she is the right person, I don't want to share my cousin's information with her. Take that!

Julie L Faith Givvers good for you!!

...

* * *

I only skim the hundred-plus comments. I do check back before turning in for the night and see nothing new. Just more responses from other adoptees and what they call donor-conceived people. I want to forget it, but the idea of another child out there is an undertow that keeps pulling me out to these posts, but I still don't "friend" Faith.

Finally, at the end of the week, I check in before the weekend. Faith has a new post for me.

Faith Givvers I found my sister.

When I click on the photograph, it takes me to this page on GoFundAFriend:

I click on the text image and then swipe to enlarge it. It doesn't make sense at first. Apparently, Faith found a GoFundAFriend site through an Internet search engine. I try to do the same search, typing in Melissa's full name. Not much. *I know what Faith must have done. She did an image search!*

I click images for the search results. *That photo is her! It matches the Ancestrology profile pic.* I click and sure enough it leads to the same text. I read:

"I am setting up this FundAFriend page for my oldest and dearest friend of 50 years. Melissa Hauben, passed away on November 20th. She was a teacher with the New York board of education, who devoted her life to working with children who have autism.

Melissa suffered from a variety of illnesses throughout her life, including Parkinson's disease, and cancer, though that did not stop her from being in the classroom. Melissa spent all of her savings on her many illnesses, leaving her without funds for a proper burial. All her family is deceased. I would appreciate any help with covering her funeral expenses. THANK YOU IN ADVANCE!"

Faith Givvers Her friend posted this two weeks after Melissa last checked her Ancestrology account.

It turns out she was a childless widow but had a very good friend, Lisa, who was making plans for her burial. I will try to reach this friend to learn more about my adoptee sister. Hugs to all adoptees reading this.

I wish we had met. Most likely we shared a birth-father, Bill Yard [photo posted in the Comments], who later became Director of Fiscal Services for NYC special needs adoptions and foster care, he says.

I feel nervous reading this. *Will anyone I know find out that I've given away more than half of my children?*

Faith Givvers I met him and he knew about me from the beginning. I also met Melissa's and my half-brother who knew about me. I don't know if our two menfolk knew about Melissa.

I cringe. *No, I didn't! I swear I didn't. I may have lied to Rémy but I was truthful to you and Kieran.*

Faith Givvers RIP, Melissa, my sweet sister.
278 Hearts   195 Comments

...

I can't read all one-hundred and ninety-five comments. The first couple dozen or so I am only looking to see if anyone is cursing me. Someone did make an off-color comment but the rest focus on Faith and Melissa never having the chance to meet. Not a single post said they weren't really sisters. Not a single post claimed Faith hadn't really lost someone.

I scrolled quite a way and then a photo of myself stops me. One of the ones from the day Faith and I met. I'm seated at the restaurant table.

Faith Givvers I see our birth-father in her. This is one of the photos I would have shared with her.

<<Image contains: Man seated at table>>

I feel a pain in my chest. It's just anxiety, I feel like I just walked into a post office and see myself on an FBI wanted poster. Should I report this photo as harassment? On what grounds? Refusing to cover for me? Sharing a photo of their shared father? I suck and I just wish this would go away.

I check to see if we have any people in common. *Kieran!*

But I can count on his silence. He will not want to hurt Rémy. I already asked him to keep this from her and he seems to have kept the silence.

...

CeCe Moore I am heartbroken for you **Faith Givvers**. I am so very very sorry.

Faith Givvers CeCe Moore, thank you. You stepped in and brought in genealogical clarity at the end which helped me immensely when I felt fogged by emotion.

I know this name: CeCe Moore. It was on a thread a few days ago, someone pointing the way for Faith. I google it and pull up and skim an article titled, "A Trailblazing Citizen Scientist of the Human Genome".

As advances in DNA technology grew, CeCe Moore and a small community of self-taught citizen-scientists helped people find immediate relatives through their own DNA.

In 2013, she became the DNA expert on the PBS docuseries, *Finding Your Roots with Henry Louis Gates, Jr.*, after Harvard professor, author, and historian Dr. Henry Louis Gates, Jr., saw one of her presentations.

CeCe Moore and other investigative genetic genealogists utilized DNA testing to catch notorious Golden State Killer Joseph DeAngelo, 73, a retired police officer who eluded authorities for decades before his arrest on April 24, 2018.

Authorities linked DNA he'd allegedly left behind at crime scenes to DNA that relatives had uploaded to GEDmatch, a site that compares DNA from multiple popular retail DNA test kits. He has since been tried and convicted. Her successful but painstaking fight to bring the Golden State Killer to justice has inspired a cohort of genealogists, many imitating her long hairdo which is parted on the side and wavy at the ends. One DNA detective claims, "We hope to take the serial out of serial killer."

Now that so many long-forgotten crimes are being solved with genetic genealogy, 'My greatest hope is that perhaps it will keep some people from committing a crime in the first place," says Moore.'"

Well, I guess they don't have to come after me! Faith seems to have moved on. But I'm feeling sad now, surprisingly sad.

...

JL Oh no... I'm very sad to wake up this morning and read about this tragic news. I'm sorry that both of you didn't get the chance to connect in the way she was obviously searching for too. ☹

...

CLK Oh Faith Givvers! I'm so sorry to hear about finding and losing your sister! It is such a strange, ambiguous and VERY REAL THING to feel tremendous loss for someone we've never even met! BUT NO SHOULDS!! They don't do anyone any good. AND YOU are doing your very best with an unnatural set-up! The loss of your sister is big enough... don't pile anything more on top! (((Big Heartfelt Hug))) just for you!

...

Meg Kearney❤
Faith Givvers Thanks, Meg.

I think that's the poet who won the PEN award and the Washington Prize! She was adopted?

...

Demi M Oh no Faith, this is horrible news. This is the perfect example as to why Adoptees need all their true identity and family information from the start. Makes me really mad. I hope your sister's friend will become yours. ❤

Faith Givvers Can you imagine, and I have, if we were able to meet easily once we were legal adults? Thanks to you, Demi Morgan, to my birth-father, and to my half-brother I have info on our paternal side I could have given her. She might have met them as well. Her best friend, Lisa, mentioned somehow having gotten her OBC before they were unsealed in NYC.

Demi M Faith Givvers, maybe her good friend will know more about it or know others that knew the most about her and connect with you.

Faith Givvers We hope to meet later in the spring as I will drive or fly to see her where she's moved in Florida.

* * *

After Rémy goes to bed, I walk quietly out to the passage next to the living room. I've turned this short hallway into a study. Once the laptop screen is glowing, I find Faith again. As soon as I find her social feed, a small video begins to stream with a doleful instrumental playing quietly underneath.

Faith Givvers This is my 17 SECOND REUNION VIDEO

1. This is my first glimpse of my sister: Ancestrology-DNA results.
2. She's a widowed, childless adoptee on a poignant search.
3. I took this photo of our biological father the one time I met him.
4. This photo of Melissa shows their resemblance.
5. I am holding a gift for my sister.
6. Her name is included for the *kaddish* prayer this sabbath. And for every November 20th, the anniversary of her passing...
7. I finally found you.

89 Hearts 18 Comments
...

I scroll through condolence message after condolence

message, each time morbidly popping open the list of emojis to confirm there's no name I recognize.

Faith I don't even know why I, and others, waited. A few years ago, I tried one test kit and got no real matches so I ignored advice to try other kits. If only I had listened...

MS We waited, I think, because we felt as if we were betraying someone.

Faith Hmmm. Who? Birth-parents? Adoptive parents? Grandparents?

MS Faith Givvers the ones who fed and clothed us.

Faith MS, that would certainly be true for some, I bet. I remember feeling guilty after my birthmom called years ago because I suddenly had biological ancestors but my Mom still didn't have biological descendants. I don't know how rational that feeling was...but it's what I felt. Along with being thrilled.

RKT She would have loved knowing she had a sister!!!

SKF So sorry closed records kept her from you. May she Rest In Peace.

...

* * *

I have trouble sleeping each night for almost the whole next year. During my waking hours there are times I think about telling Kieran about Melissa but bat the thought aside, one time when I'm alone even swatting the air like an irritable old man.

Maybe once or twice I think of reaching for Faith. Not posting, no, reaching out by email but decide against it. Maybe Faith will reach out to Kieran again and then I'll just let it play out. As far as I know she doesn't or Kieran doesn't tell me. We all guard the taboo, eh?

As the days grow shorter, so does my temper and I catch myself bickering with Rémy. I lag in keeping up with my usual hobbies, wood carving and computer-based drawing. I gaze with growing sorrow at the trivial leaf storms that dance their way along the sidewalk below our apartment. It becomes almost unbearable by the week before Thanksgiving. To snap myself out of this funk – I tell myself it is boredom – I go back online and look at Faith's account.

I see someone has posted a link to a live Allman Brothers performance of "Sweet Melissa". Predictable and I don't bother watching. But I brace myself and a few posts down is a Nashville video "Never Comin' Down". In it, Keith Urban plays both bartender and guitar in a club that welcomes every gender and sexuality, I guess what they call an LGBTQ+ inclusive video. Faith posted it with the intro that "Melissa dedicated this song to her late partner, her person with whom she lived and loved since even before marriage equality".

Melissa had a life partner. I feel a rush of relief, gratitude.

* * *

I'm scrolling a day or so later when I see the image of a young woman's face appear. Faith has posted it. A sketch by Ophelia? Not quite like her. The strokes are angrier than the style I remember from that summer. It is sketched in thick red and eggplant pastels on heavy tan paper. Ophelia emphasizes certain features with deft strokes of charcoal. Why the black overlay? Comments are already appearing.

Faith This is a picture my birth-mother drew for me of me! My birth-mother sketched this picture of me and then highlighted the features of my birth-father as she remembered them in it. A curious but priceless gift. I have a relationship with Ophelia but not Bill.

The story behind this picture is one that I realize now was quietly courageous.

My birthmother drew this of me the first time we met, trying to highlight the features that reminded her of my father so she could "give" him to me.

...

I pause at the next one. It must be someone who knows both Faith and this other daughter I apparently had. It must be the friend who raised money for Melissa's funeral.

LLP I like this picture, you remind me of your sister Melissa. I think it's your eyes. I miss her so much.

Faith Givvers I miss her too. A different kind of loss. Thank you for being so welcoming and sharing a little bit of her with me, L.

They're both rubbing it in. I never claimed to be proud of what I did. On the other hand, they're not expecting me to see this so what they write isn't meant for me. Faith does have my eyes. Eyes and ears like Kieran's.

...

CCM What a beautiful way for her to share what she remembers of your birth-father as he was then.

...

Faith Givvers Thank you. It's taken me a long time to put it out there because it is too poignant to imagine her alone in her flat reaching back in time to remember him then.

Ouch. But not ouch enough for me to open up a can of worms by telling Rémy. She'd want to bring Faith in, just like Rémy did all those years ago when Ophelia was pregnant. One part of me wants to be right there with Faith and another wants to run in the other direction.

Faith doesn't need me.

* * *

A few months pass and then during another Covid shelter-in-place, a new thread pops up. An apparent stranger named Jon M----- is posting back and forth with Faith.

1:37 AM

Jon Hi Faith, not to disturb you in any way... if you're still searching for info & details for your half-sister Melissa, perhaps I can assist. Melissa & I dated & were engaged in college & we knew one another quite well but, we never married. In turn, I knew her parents Charlotte & Bob. I moved West 7 years ago, now in Scottsdale. I had no clue Melissa had passed away until this evening while I was researching related folks @ AHRC on-line due to another death in my family = a cousin Melissa knew.

Anyway, my heart goes out to those who seek family info. So, if you wish to speak or text, I offer you my cell # for either. I am Jon M-----. Since I'm in AZ I'm currently on Pacific time – 3 hours behind Eastern time. I welcome your call or text any day after 12:00 noon 10 or 11:00 pm. Likewise, I'm sure I can dig out a photo or two if you wish from a rather extensive family archive. Be well, Jon

3:29 PM

Jon Melissa's upstate back yard with my sister's Husky pup.

I look at the photo of the dark-haired woman, wearing a shag cut and a short navy-blue winter jacket that cinches at the waist. She is in jeans and beat up sneakers bending over a blue-eyed huskie pup. Then the recognition hits me! She looks like – her frame – like that girl I dated at Cooper Union downtown. Definitely like Suzie.

11:49 AM

Faith Hello!

Faith I haven't been on this account in a while. Thanks for writing! I'd love to know anything and everything you want to share. How did you find me???

Faith I "found" Melissa through Ancestrology results but she passed away a few days after she last checked her account. I signed up only a few days after that. Just missed each other!

2:32 PM

Jon Wow, thought I'd never hear from you! Faith, your note is quite welcome.

OK, so, I finally had time to peruse your post AND all those marvelous replies/suggestions...

[Several photos of Melissa with small groups of people.] WOW. Know what? This, my dear, is what good deeds are made of!

Notice the snapshot of Melissa with Professor Dennis & Jane Lou? Enlarge Melissa's face AND THAT is the flawless image of your dear sister, heart & soul. That was her inner, relaxed happy self. It's both innocence & calm and hopefully what carried her on her journey.

...

Summer, 2023

I see a red alert pop up to let me know I have a direct message. I open it but then cut my Internet connection, almost superstitiously, to prevent a real-time conversation. *I know this is childish but I don't want to be put on the spot.* Offline, I see it is a note from Faith.

Faith Givvers Bill, you have another daughter. Um. Congratulations!!

Perhaps you knew this all along and withheld the information from Kieran and me. Perhaps you are just discovering her through these posts.

There is no grave marker but three kind people gave her to me in another way.

I found her best friend and flew to meet her (and an old friend from here who happened to have moved nearby there) this summer. We planned to meet for breakfast and instead spent six hours together sharing her best friend/my sister/your first-born child.

I found her childhood babysitter who told me she'd paid for Melissa's dental care when cancer treatment ravaged the inside of my sweet Melissa's mouth.

Her former college fiancé found me online and even mailed me a piece of jewelry she gave him long ago. It was a keychain of sailing locks, something she liked to hold.

These kind people each shared their image of Melissa and the three images came together like a hologram to give me a three-dimensional image of my sister, the first daughter of yours placed for adoption.

~ Faith

I shut the laptop on Faith's note and quickly leave the room as though I might be followed.

~ 17 ~

FAITH 2024, NEW JERSEY

Faith and Susan sat on a wood bench against the marble wall and under the vaulted ceiling of the old courthouse. Their trial had moved here from the new justice complex across the street that was having computer hub issues. At the end of the hallway a mural depicted a blindfolded Themis, one the Greek Titans, holding the familiar scales of Justice and Law. Cherubs and satyrs danced around her in brushstrokes that were clearly the work of a school art class. Bronze wall sconces and leaded windows managed to hold onto their dignity regardless, and made the white marble floors glow.

The Birth-Fathers' Club test case was in session and the judge had requested that overflow wait in this lobby. Every bench was taken. It had already been two hours, but Ted Landtsman stepped out to tell them the judge would go late and adjourn around one.

That triggered Faith's disappointment anew that Bill

hadn't testified in the lower court like the other birth-fathers.

Faith and Susan thanked Ted.

After the courtroom door closed behind him Faith turned back to her notepad. She'd been using the time for work on the documentary – because as he'd explained to the Birth-Fathers' Club meeting a few months ago – both Ted and their adversaries would fight this all the way to the U.S. Supreme Court. In other words, Faith knew today's outcome mattered but it would only be the beginning and not the end of their filming. She spent the time in the lobby writing up notes for a filming schedule.

FF Documentary filming schedule notes from FG:
Tokyo & Kamakura shots

> Young couples praying for conception and safe pregnancy; new families offering gratitude: *Suitengu* Shrine, Tokyo.

> Miniature stone children placed in memory of lost pregnancies: *Jizou-do* at *Hasedera* Temple, Kamakura.

> B-roll: Tokyo fertility clinic; petri dish; homes for surrogate mothers and unwed mothers in India, Thailand, or United States; Kamakura surfers, etc.

NYC shots

> Birth-Fathers' Club meeting at office of Ted Landtsman, Esq. NOTE: Hire add'l crew to cover the

building's loading dock where Tony Silvio's entourage will enter to avoid attention.

B-roll: mist rising from NYC manhole covers; squirrels [!] – *Tokyo insists they are "exotic"*; *gaijin* babies in lower Manhattan; and the southern District of New York judicial complex facades.

Albany, state capital of NY shots

Get press permit/film inside courtroom/confirm sound engineer

Fans mobbing Tony Silvio emerging from a black stretch

B-roll: blindfolded goddess of justice holding scales; Courthouse murals; marble stairs

Washington, D.C. shots

Street interviews with donor-conceived and adoptee activists; reactions hearing ruling;

B-roll: Cherry blossoms; Supreme Court exterior; Japanese embassy; the Kennedy Center.

Stock footage: Duet iconic Supreme Court confirmation images of a composed KBJ v weeping Brett Cavanaugh; Duet Fred Greenman, Esq. and Georgia "the Baby Thief" Tann.

When Faith was done re-reading this list, Susan turned to her and said, "Hey, it's like the Tom Stoppard play, *Rosencrantz and Guildenstern*, where Hamlet and the rest of the troop are swooping in and out. In the court cases we adoptees and DCPs are minor characters, although, well, I appreciate the birth-fathers helping us out now just like the birth-mothers did before. But this actually does *not* feel empowering."

Faith's heart flinched as this new thought layered on top of her powerlessness to charm her birth-father into a relationship. Even though Bill agreed to meet her. Even though he worked in the adoption field. She put the list away and stretched while she figured out how she wanted to answer Susan.

"So, you're saying we're sitting here like Rosencrantz and Guildenstern backstage. We're the minor players in the court case just like they are the minor players in *Hamlet*," and then Faith struggled with the next thought, "If the Birth-Fathers' Club are Hamlet trying to avenge wrong through their landmark case..."

"Right! Keep going..."

"Okay," said Faith, "Legally there's our same powerlessness from the adoption contract. It changed my life completely, cut me off from Bill's and Ophelia's families, introduced me to my adoptive family. I had no power to do or undo it, for better or worse."

"Yes, even today we're sitting out in the hallway even though adoptees and donor-conceived people are the ones with the most at stake with the ruling...Well, I mean the courtroom was overflowing and they needed to get as many birth-fathers inside as possible for the optics. I know," Susan said.

"It's important and I'm grateful to each one of them, but yeah, we're sitting offstage through hours of it all. *Waiting for Godot*, as my mother called it. Just as tossed by chance as the bit players Rosencrantz and Guildenstern..."

"Look what I pulled up," said Susan, "Samuel Beckett, the Irish playwright, was considered an absurdist."

"Is what we're doing absurdist? Or is it redemption? Quick!" asked Faith, "Thirty-second quiz. You have five seconds to answer the question or you forfeit. Perfect score is...is...fifteen!"

"Does that mean fifteen questions, one point each?" said Susan.

"I can only tell you once we're done..."

"Absurdist!" Susan laughed.

"No, just a sec. See, some questions have more than one right answer and some questions have no right answers," said Faith.

Susan tipped her head and smiled, waiting.

Faith was typing furiously and then called out: "Is it absurdist or is it redemption? 1. Having to be grateful for something I was told doesn't matter and I should forget."

"Absurdist!" Susan called out.

"2. It is legal to marry your biological mother, brother, sister, or father, if you're an adoptee or DCP," said Faith.

"Absurdist!" answered Susan.

"3. As an aggressive, thick-skinned member of the NYC press corps, I still thought it was 'inappropriate' to ask questions about my origins."

Susan shook her head sympathetically, "Absurdist!"

"4. Some people who want children can't have them and other people who can have them don't want them," Faith read off her device.

"Absurdist!" said Susan.

"5. I think of the trope that adoption is supposed to 'save' me and contrast it to the reality of having a birth-father willing to raise me. Add to that my adoptive father's behavior, I didn't deserve that," said Faith.

This time Susan responded quietly.

"Absurdist."

Faith made a few quick keystrokes before continuing, "6. But I also think 'I didn't deserve that' when I think of the early travel to Japan I got to experience, thanks to my maternal adoptive grandfather's generosity or the college education I received on my adoptive father's dime, or the fact that the agency placed me with a Yale-educated mother in the heart of the American crafts movement."

"And then after the funeral for your uncle in Virginia..."

"Yes! We go to the Smithsonian to ask about Mom's necklace only but instead find a whole exhibit of works by many of the family friends I knew as a child (my incredible adoptive heritage) and then right upstairs an exhibit on Native American crafts (my hidden birth heritage)! Both on display at the Smithsonian!" said Faith.

"Redemptive!" responded Susan.

"7. I had to pay a third party to learn my personal heritage. Who pays someone to learn their own mother's or father's names?" said Faith.

"Absurdist!" answered Susan.

"8. I was always being told I was 'not really Jewish' because my adoptive mother was Christian and then it turns out my maternal blood great-uncle was the Chief Rabbi for the British Empire!"

"Hah, take that! Redemptive," replied Susan.

"9. Now that I learn about my Cherokee, Choctaw and Mohawk ancestry I get to hear THAT SAME STUFF, like I'm 'not really Native'," said Faith.

"Absurdist! But you know where that's coming from, right? Someone who already has White privilege turns around and wants to claim jobs that were meant for someone who knows Native culture. Anyway, TIME. I need a break," said Susan. She stretched her legs in front of her, ankles still crossed.

"Okay, break, then I've got six more questions," said Faith.

Susan stood up and stretched her arms, then gestured for Faith to continue.

Faith scrolled down and read out, "Is it absurdist or redemptive? 10. Did I mention that BOTH Indigenous Americans and Jews are each only two-percent of this country's population and worry existentially about their numbers while simultaneously turning away some adoptees and DCPs with Indigenous or Jewish heritage?"

"Absurdist!" called out Susan.

Faith scrolled down her notes and then read, "11. Some unwed mothers gave their infants away out of shame for having them and then years later decline to have them back out of shame for giving them away."

Susan answered, "Absurdist!"

"12. The man who gave away his first born and then his next daughter went on to work in the field of adoption and fostercare for New York City," said Faith.

"Redemptive!" said Susan.

"Hmmm, okay, the judges will give you that one," said Faith. Then she continued, "13. It's not unusual for the ancestor-less adoptee or their spouse to become the family genealogist, not only because they've gotten good at reunioncraft but because they feel called to it."

Susan answered with a slow smile, "Redemptive!"

Faith said impishly, "14. Just when scared, secretive, or control-freaky people turn to anonymous and no-contact donors, donor-conceived people discover adoptee allies and DNA tests."

"Redemptive!" called Susan.

"15. The adoption agency that once sealed away my

Indigenous heritage has also testified in the lower courts in this case *in favor* of heritage equality," Faith said thoughtfully.

"Redemptive!" Susan said and relaxed against the marble wall of the courthouse.

Part 5

From the FF documentary:

FAITH

"Prizes I've brought back from this quest? I carried shame that I didn't even realize. Now I've released that shame enough to convince Ryuji Kato to cover the Birth-fathers' Club test case."

SOLOMON

"Prizes? Now, that's a good word for it. Prizes from this reunion include knowing I gave the world a beautiful, caring daughter as its citizen. It's when adoption works right: childless couples have a child who loves them and a child has parents who love them, Book of Malachi."

SUSAN

"For me the prizes are finding our stories within stories: Pearl in *The Scarlet Letter*, Moses, his birth- and adoptive parents in the oral traditions for *Exodus*, and Sol's using Judah, the first male donor, to get an entire room to understand the long-term obligations to DCPs."

~ 18 ~

SUSAN 2024, FLORIDA

For their second in-person visit, Susan and Sol agreed that she would fly down to his condo in Florida, arriving late Friday afternoon. Other than David, Susan told only Faith about the trip. She had flown to her birth-country and met her birth-mother ten years earlier in Thailand. Now she was going to visit her birth-father in his every-day habitat.

As telling as the similarity of their thumbs, which Susan pointed out as he turned the steering wheel onto Yamato Drive, was the way both of them tilted their head when they were listening. The trip from the airport should have given them plenty of time to talk about more, but instead they lapsed into silence, both very aware of the presence of the other.

Her birth-father's town, Deerfield Beach, was one of the south Florida towns located on the sheetflow between the Kissimmee River basin and the coast. In fact, the landscape reminded her of a cross between Scotland and a manicured Southeast Asian resort: flat expanses of turf surrounded by the flora of palms, winter-blooming bushes and tropical birds. Both Florida and Thailand harbored orchids on hardwood land hammocks.

The difference was her birth-country was ripe with seeds and fruit, some kind of metaphor, she supposed. She wondered why she didn't see fleshy orchids or jasmine or tropical fruit trees in this landscape, too. On the ride from the airport, she asked Sol about this. He explained that condominium boards forbade jasmine because some residents objected to its redolent perfume. Years ago, fruit bearing trees were also banned and then uprooted because they attracted wasps and other wildlife. Also, their seeds could lead to growth outside established garden borders. Susan couldn't help thinking that was a metaphor, too. For sowing wild oats of the human kind. Her birth-father, when Susan commented on it, didn't seem to read anything into it.

In fact, when they pulled into the driveway her birth-father commented on "the dirty tree" out front whose leaves would yellow and fall on the lawn and roof during storms. So she stepped out of his car into a barely scented afternoon and took in the tough-grassed lawns that gave no hints of either fruitfulness or ferment.

She asked him about plans for that evening.

"I would be honored if you'd read something I'm working on. Feel free to edit. They've asked me to give a little talk on next week's Bible portion," Sol said.

"My pleasure. I wish I were going to be here next week to attend that service."

"You'd certainly be welcome. I'm going to work from Genesis 37:1 - 40:23. But come in, I'll show it to you after supper. Let's get you settled."

~ 19 ~

SOLOMON 2024, FLORIDA

I set out some salads and a sandwich platter while Susan and Shotgun played on the living room rug. Susan found his squeaky toy behind the sofa. When I asked her about drinks, we discovered a shared appreciation of pink lemonade. It felt profound. After lunch I took her on a tour of my tiny condo. When we reached the side room there is one thing I knew she had to see.

"See that up there?"

Hanging on a peg, next to a fishing cap and an old set of car keys. I show her my old green beret. The felt is pilled and the leather of the black band is starting to crack.

"It's beat up, it's sewn up. But I'll never wash it because I always say, let the blood, sweat and tears stay on it."

She straightens her shoulders. We just stand there, almost at attention, facing the wall of old photos and the old beret.

She's a smart girl, I think she caught that. It is one of those moments, you know, and the amount of emotion is more than you'd expect from these old soldier's eyes. Proud, relieved, fond, sad unto longing, but mostly proud. For the men and for my daughter who, good Lord, had tracked me down.

Something good from the war.

* * *

After we both get up to clear the table and load the dishwasher, I show Susan my work area. I look away when I explain, "This morning was probably the hundredth time I've read this week's Bible portion under this same Tiffany lamp at my old mahogany desk but this time I'm actually weeping to think how much meaning it holds for me now."

Susan puts down a small clementine she was peeling.

"This is definitely the R-rated part of the Bible, Susan," I warn her before continuing, "Tamar's husband has died and she's still living with his clan in her father-in-law's tents, almost like a captive because her father-in-law, Judah, won't allow her to remarry."

So, I open the heavy book and start reading.

"*Genesis 38:14 'And Tamar changed out of the garments of her widowhood, and covered herself with a veil, and wrapped herself, and sat in the entrance of Enaim,.... 15 When Judah saw her, he thought her to be a harlot; for she had covered her face.*

16 And he turned unto her by the way, and said: 'Come, I pray thee, let me come in unto thee'; for he knew not that she was his daughter-in-law.

And she said, 'What wilt thou give me, that thou mayest come in unto me?'

17 And he said: 'I will send thee a kid of the goats from the flock.'

And she said: 'Wilt thou give me a pledge, till thou send it?'

18 And he said: 'What pledge shall I give thee?'

And she said: 'Thy signet and thy cord, and thy staff that is in thy hand.'

And he gave them to her, and came in unto her, and she conceived by him.

19 And she arose, and went away, and put off the veil from her and changed back into the garments of her widowhood. 20 And Judah sent the kid of the goats by the hand of his friend the Adullamite, to receive the pledge from the woman's hand; but he found her not.

21 Then he asked the men of her place, saying: 'Where is the harlot that was at Enaim by the wayside?'

And they said: 'There hath been no harlot here.'

22 And he returned to Judah, and said: 'I have not found her; and also the men of the place said: 'There hath been no harlot here.'....

24 And it came to pass about three months after, that it was told Judah, saying: 'Tamar thy daughter-in-law hath played the harlot; and moreover, behold, she is with child by harlotry.'

And Judah said; 'Bring her forth, and let her be burnt,'" and here I make sure Susan is looking at the text by pointing.

"I'm following along," Susan says.

"Okay. *25 When she was brought forth, she sent to her father-in-law, saying: 'By the man whose these are am I with child'; and she said: 'Discern, I pray thee, whose are these, the signet, and the cords, and the staff.'*

26 And Judah acknowledged them....

I stop and look up.

I can see Susan is stunned, "Wow. Just 'wow'—the world's first birth-father? I can't tell if he's one of the good guys or one of the bad guys in the Bible."

"Well," I consider, "through one of their twins Judah and Tamar are supposed to be ancestors of the Messiah. And Judah manned up in the end."

"What are you going to say?"

"All in all, the Bible set the bar pretty low for mortal fathers. No wonder everyone prays instead to a Heavenly Father."

"Interesting."

"No, no, that's just between you and me, there's no point in my being cynical. I've still got a way to go. Well, look. Basically, if there were close to four million people placed for adoption between the end of World War II and the legalization of birth control in the United States —that's one number out there—then there are four million birth-fathers out there. Maybe some in our congregation. It's time for them to lobby their state to give those adoptees access to their records. The United Kingdom restored adult adoptees' access to their original birth certificates back in the mid-seventies and the British Isles didn't sink back into the ocean. It's time more men were like Judah and manned up."

"Get ready for some lively conversation in the social hall afterwards. You've become a good advocate."

"I could do this forever," I say.

Susan peers briefly over my Bible with its faint whiff of rice paper. It crackles as I smooth the next page. My water glass bends the glow of the desk lamp's light toward her. Susan takes this all in before she turns to go.

"Susan?" I say.

She turns back and reaches out one hand to give mine a squeeze before she leaves. I turn back to my draft. I want to work a quote from the Prophets in here too. I mean to tell her about it but guess I know I'll get too choked up. That Zoom call, I heard it anew when Susan and Faith and their friends read it. I've read it at Passover before, it is from the Book of Malachi.

Now, just touching my found daughter's hand, thinking of the parents who raised her too, it feels like the most important promise in the world: *'He will turn the hearts of the parents to the children and the hearts of the children to the parents before the coming of the great and awesome day of God.'"*

* * *

A few weeks later, the woman I've taken to calling my daughter flies down again. She isn't introducing me to her kids yet. Her husband stays behind with them. It is just the two of us looking at old photo albums when I lean forward and I guess I wince a little.

"What's the matter?" Susan asks.

"It's nothing," I answer but she looks at me with suspicion in her eyes. I might as well tell her.

"I'm okay. I still feel one of the bullet wounds. The one near my heart."

She is quiet for a minute. Then she looks up at me like she just remembered something, "I heard about the Defense bill and the White House. Yitzie told me a little about it."

I almost laugh. So, she is beginning to reach out to the rest of the family. I know but I ask her anyway, "Yitzie? You spoke to my sister? She likes to talk."

"She's proud of you. She also said you always mow her lawn when you come out."

"She's a widow. I like doing it," I say.

"She says you were married once and that you beat cancer? She says there is some news. That there was some investigation by the military?"

I hesitate at this one.

Susan must wonder if my humility is upbringing or genuine.

I decide to open up, "A few years back Congress ordered the Pentagon to waive the usual time limits and investigate whether there had been discrimination in the awarding of the Medal of Honor and the Distinguished

Service Cross all the way back to the Civil War. Turns out they did uncover a couple dozen veterans that never got the MoH despite qualifying. Now the Joint Chiefs are going to make sure it's awarded by the President of the United States as Commander in Chief to each and every one who got overlooked."

Susan tells me she's heard this too from Yitzie. What she wants to hear about is my end of it and she nudges me with, "Yitzie said they did give you the Distinguished Service Cross, the second highest medal for bravery awarded, but you really should have been awarded the Medal of Honor. Yitzie said, they are both given only for only actions in combat and that the Medal of Honor is the highest in the land."

It may be true, but I don't need to live in the past, I tell her.

"She said the President called you."

"Anything she didn't tell you?"

Susan can tell I'm not too upset and insists, "Come on."

"Well, it's true." I sip some coffee to wet my lips before continuing, "The President himself called me here at home. Oh, boy!" It's only the phone but I'm still shaking my head and smiling.

"It's true then!"

I nod and tell her, "I fell to my knees and said, 'Oh, my God, what have I done?' The President tells me 'It's all good.' He tells me about the Pentagon investigation of thousands of files to identify wrongful denials of the Congressional Medal of Honor and the Distinguished Service Cross which he, as President, will now award. I can't believe it. The President, he's saying, 'Be cool, be cool, be cool.'"

Susan laughs and taps me on the shoulder, "I am so proud of you. You're a war hero! I couldn't have imagined any of this."

I decide to take a gamble, "They're inviting me up to the White House East Room next month. I know you have your kids, but—"

"Are you asking me—us—to be there?"

"Yes, I am." The next words are so mushy they stick in my throat, "It's only good if you share it," and I mean it.

There's a lot of chapters already past in my life and now I'm alone. I'm okay with that but I'll be feeling better and better with this new daughter. I'm more excited about this award because of her.

I try to explain, "I want to share it with you and David. You and the kids are part of my family, too. And bring your adoptive parents, too. Why not? They're my clan, too, now."

I surprised myself with that last one.

Susan can't stop her tears. It is something to see. She says, "You better believe we'll be there."

Those words were as good as the call from the President himself. Maybe even better.

~ 20 ~

FAITH 2025, NEW YORK CITY

FF Documentary notes from FG:

RK negotiating distribution & marketing.

FG to negotiate credits and concert footage of old Allman Brothers; America; Aztec Camera/Roddy Frame; Buddy Holly; C.A. Feissner [out of Sendai, Japan]; Cat Stevens; Chris Whitley; Crosby, Stills & Nash; Darryl McDaniels/Run DMC; Diana Ross & The Supremes; Drake; Everly Brothers; Firefall; Glenn Miller; Joni Mitchell; Keith Urban; Lou Reed; the Marvelettes; Pusha T; Robbie Robertson/The Band; Roger Daltrey; Rolling Stones; Rod Stewart; Steven Tyler; Screamin' Jay Hawkins; Sheryl Crow; Tim McGraw; Tom Petty; Tommy Tutone; The Tony Silvio Project; and, Traffic.

Post-production – editing/motion graphics/audio design/translation & dubbing/mastering.

Faith and Susan were having lunch near Susan's work at the Argot. Not the diner where Susan met Sol, but a sushi shop with broiled cod like Momoya's but at half the price. It had been over two months since they saw each other.

Toward the end of the hour, they pushed their plates aside and were finishing coffees when Faith said, "You know, Susan, there were a lot of personal fireworks for me to discovering proof of my Indigenous family, with all the family trees on Ancestrology that matched to me and also pointed to Minnie, the Cherokee/Choctaw, and Dinah, the Haudenosaunee ancestors. The reunioncraft of the relatives on my missing paternal side suddenly took me from blank slate to collage."

"Collage. That's funny, I like it."

"But there's a genealogist on my maternal side too. A lot less fireworks because Ophelia and I actually have a relationship," said Faith. "And, by the way, I think our relationship has finally grown out of adolescence; I no longer roll my eyes at everything the poor woman says."

"Amen to that."

"Hey."

"Sorry. In your text you said you were going to tell me about a dinner. You had 'an unsuspected but long-known cousin'. 'Treasure'? That's a great name!" said Susan.

"Yeah, and she didn't choose it as a stage name, her parents really named her Treasure. I've known her for years in the community. Between her name and her wonderful smile, one of those light-up-the-room smiles, everyone who meets her remembers her. Long story short, I'm planning the next trip to visit Ophelia in London. The family genealogist has a list-serv so I ask on it about the UK cousins. In one of the answers, I notice Treasure's name for the first time! Turns out she's a second cousin once removed. The best part is that as soon as we realize the connection, she invites us over to dinner. And we've stayed in touch, seen each other a couple times since," said Faith.

"So, your 'unsuspected but long-known cousin' didn't make you wait years or meet you once and tell you 'it's all bullshit.' You deserve someone like this, finally! How was dinner at their house?" said Susan.

"It's a cute house, like walking into a diorama. Treasure and her husband had her older sister Rebecca there too. When I looked around, I realized it was a relinquished person's dream come true: the home was stacked with family photo albums. I don't know if they just got them out for me or if they usually have them on the coffee tables, but the albums were full of old family portraits. New pictures of their four grown children and grandchildren filled every shape of refrigerator magnet. Their grown children and grandchildren live around the country. The couple must be in their eighties but they travel to visit several times a year," Faith said.

Faith drank some tea before continuing. "Then it gets goose-bumps interesting at the end of the evening when Rebecca asks me to repeat my adoptive family's name."

"Goose-bumps interesting?"

"Yes! Rebecca asked, 'Givvers? An Eddy Givvers?' and I tell her that was my Grandpa," said Faith. "Then Rebecca says, 'Eddy, Eddy! What a funny, lovely man,' then she seemed to consider something and blurts out, 'That family was different, not really part of the community' which was absolutely true."

"What do you mean?" Susan asked cautiously.

People had commented about Faith's adoptive family over the years. It was unusual for a Jewish family that soon after the Holocaust not to seek the community of a synagogue. Faith used to explain that she was fourth-generation unaffiliated. Faith gave a shrug and then continued, "Rebecca says, 'They gave their son and daughter such traditional names,' and then, Susan, she says the names of my adoptive father and aunt! 'My husband may have gone to high school with your father. I remember he did business with Eddy.' Talk about synchronicity," Faith said.

Rebecca's husband, Dan, who was not with them at dinner that night, had indeed graduated from high school in Newark with Faith's adoptive father. Faith called him later in the week and he was happy to speak about Grandpa Eddy but reluctant to talk to her about her adoptive father. Instead he gave her the phone number of another classmate who was equally taciturn other than to say, "I never really got him."

"Yeah, well," said Susan.

"And, Susan, remember my cousin Sharon, Ophelia's niece? She texted me with a request recently," said Faith. "It went 'I can't reach our Uncle Roger and he didn't send my mother his usual birthday card this year, would you track him down?'"

"'Would you track him down', Faith?" Susan laughed and clapped her hands, "'Would you track him down'! Do you think maybe it was a way for her to make you feel somewhat included in the family?"

"Welcomed in? She seems like that kind of person, yes," said Faith. "Well, I found him through his girlfriend. He was staying at her place and she had the simplest explanation, 'Roger is fine, it's just age-appropriate decrepitude.' I love these people. I love their sense of humor."

Susan gave her miso soup a dainty sip before asking with a twinkle, "Isn't Roger the one who said –"

"Yes, yes, the first time I spoke to him years ago, Roger told me, 'We aren't a very close family; we only get together *once* a year on Thanksgiving.' I never told you the rest, Susan. A while later I spoke to Janice – remember his and Ophelia's sister? – who very, very seriously explains, 'We're a very close family; we get together *every* year on Thanksgiving.'"

"Oh, noooooo."

"You know how they say you can pick your friends but you can't pick your family? I'd pick my cousin Jonathan and his wife Kristen for either category. And our kids! Our youngest finally has a family member the same age! Kristen and Jonathan are the ones we spend the most time with, she's the editor and he's the musician," said Faith before adding thoughtfully, "And Mary, Jonathan's Mom and Roger's ex, was the first to welcome me into her home...

"Actually, she welcomes a lot of people on a regular basis. One time I was there, Susan, when Mary explains, 'We're eating outside today because all the Ugandan refugees are still asleep in the dining room.' It's how they roll," Faith laughed.

~ 21 ~

BILL 2025, NEW YORK CITY

Only three years after finding Faith, I find myself tiring easily. I joke with Rémy that at least I have no trouble falling asleep.

I am lying. Actually, I have trouble staying awake. The two problems are different, I am learning, and I don't sleep well, just often.

One morning I probe and find swollen lymph nodes under my jaw. Rémy notices that I've developed a cough. Neither hurt so I shrug it off. Then when I wake with night sweats, we joke that I must be going through menopause as a man in my early seventies. Finally, when I start having shortness of breath and a fever Rémy makes a doctor's appointment.

Non-Hodgkin's lymphoma.

Sitting up becomes an effort. I find myself dozing off when my son, Kieran, comes to visit. He and I don't try hard to reach out to Faith. Well, I do send her an email but it bounces back. Her phone number is listed, she's told me. I still have it somewhere. It is too much now – to meet again. I never did answer her note on social about Melissa. I want to sleep.

Maybe Kieran will reach back to Faith some time. I can let go now, knowing he has Faith as a sibling. Sounds like she has a good life anyway. I do print out the copy of that long-ago letter I wrote to her. This time I don't tear it up. I put it in an envelope and write "Kieran" on the outside. He will find Faith.

~ 22 ~

FINDING FAITH

"Please give this to Faith," is the only thing written on the slip of paper Clay Dennen pulled out of the envelope that came addressed to Faith Givvers, c/o The Birth-Fathers' Club P. O. Box.... It is signed "Kieran". Faith has finished her term as treasurer so Clay opens it expecting an invoice.

Accompanying the terse note are several sheaths of folded paper. Clay unfolds them enough to see that they are signed in what he judges is a man's hand although he does not read the contents. He finds Faith's number in the directory and gives her a call.

When Clay explains what has been sent, she says simply, "I bet I know what it is, Clay. My birth-father told me he ripped it up. I always wanted to see it. I don't care what's in it, I want to know the truth."

Clay forwards it on. Three days later, Faith pulls eight sheets of heavy stock with old-fashioned watermarks out of a double-bond envelope. She reads the long letter straight through from beginning to end.

Dear Faith,

You asked me about the significance of the day we met, which I can understand given your different upbringing and my wearing a cross of ashes.

Yes, it was Ash Wednesday the day I picked to meet. No significance there although you sought one. We spoke on Sunday. I had morning meetings Monday and Tuesday so it was really only because it was the soonest I could see you. Still, I'd agree it was the longest three days of my life.

I'm definitely a lapsed Catholic. That morning the lines outside St. Patrick's were as good as "a happening" so I waited on line. My wearing the ashes that morning we met had no significance. I like the architecture of that church. On the other hand, maybe I did feel the old tug of ceremony, something to mark the first meeting with my first child. I suppose you being raised outside the Church it wouldn't have occurred to you to go inside as I did. So, in that sense the years of catechism still have their hold on me.

I didn't fight hard enough for you. In fact, to be truthful, it was my fiancé Rémy who said we must raise you; you are my child. Many times, she's been my conscience. Maybe that's why I couldn't tell her that you've resurfaced. She'd want to include you. I have that same impulse. Right after you and I had brunch I called my son, Kieran, and invited him out for a scotch. I told him everything. What I know of you. The affair during his parents' engagement. It was a conversation between men. He didn't say much but I expect you'll meet some day.

I can't believe I have three grandkids in New Jersey. My first response is happiness. Then I pause and know that I can't claim them just by saying that, I realize it. They belong to you and your adoptive parents, but if you or they ever, ever need anything I'll do whatever I can. Maybe it's not too late to somehow play a role in your lives, with deference to the man who raised you in my stead, your adoptive father.

By now, after seeing your own forthrightness, a gentler version of my bluntness, I can imagine you trying to ask the unspoken. I was the father who didn't fight for you, never went to court to try and halt it. Later in this letter or in a next letter you deserve my thinking out loud why. I will try to walk you (and me) through why.

You made an observation about my working in adoption. Yes, the connection to Robert J. Lifton and Betty Jean Lifton is through teaching their kids, but that's not what made me read her memoir. I knew you were a daughter. The first book of Betty Jean's that I read was "Memoirs of an Adopted Daughter".

I am furious with Ophelia and with myself for letting her get pregnant; this is not the same thing as regretting for a single moment that you have life. I am glad you are alive. But I was not willing to submit to a shotgun wedding, to spend the rest of my life with a woman I barely knew and did not love, nor to jilt the woman who trusted me while she was away on sabbatical, my wife Rémy.

I called your mother a lost soul, but what was I doing entering into an affair while engaged? The truth about myself is I was a lost soul who recognized another lost soul. Then I used that connection not to protect her but to take advantage of her.

I had no idea that I had saved this secret spot deep within my heart reserved for you and you alone. It was clear to me at our meeting that I was in undefined territory. I didn't have a clue. To say I had questions was an understatement. What was this mixture of feelings I was having? The books didn't cover this mix. I just wanted to hold you, touch you and not let go. It seemed so right and yet wrong at the same time. I could see that this having a long-lost daughter wasn't going to be a slam dunk.

I was as lost as I had ever been in my life. I felt embarrassed for how I felt but couldn't put my finger on why. It was like instant love with all those complicated feelings that are intertwined with that act. This feeling was so strong it was a little uncomfortable. I thought: "I can't control this." Finally, the rush-hour commuters around us broke the spell and we never embraced.

Books don't have much to say about birth-fathers

and I found I was identifying more with birth-mothers than I expected.

I know my body contributed half the blueprint but not the cellular material to build the fetus that became you. That original material for the most part has been modified and or replaced over the last few decades. I did, however, along with Ophelia, create a mold from which you were formed into this physical person you are today. I believe that the part of me that sent the directions to start the process of creating you recognizes you today outside of my conscience mind.

A bond that can't be broken. Call it inherent memory or what you might, it is what it is.

I did visit you in the hospital when you were born, but I didn't check in with the adoption agency to ask about you. Ophelia checked out of the hospital while you were still there. I was able to find you because you were listed as "Baby Girl Yard". You were in the intensive care nursery because of neo-natal jaundice so I never held you. You said when Ophelia asked to see you a social worker or nurse told her you had already been adopted. They misled her into believing she couldn't hold you while she was still in the hospital. Maybe they were afraid she'd get it together and keep you. Maybe they were right. You will never know that.

Either the agency or she lied. Someone could and should have held you. I remember seeing you. They had you under special lights to reduce your bilirubin count. Not in those days but—you'll see something on a slow news night on the local news broadcasts where volunteers go in to hold newborns that are very sick. Retirees, often, they'll put one of those hospital gowns over their street clothes and sit in a rocker at the hospital and just hold and rock these babies. They talk to them or sing to them. If they're awake they'll hold them in their eyes as well as their arms. I hope there was someone like that there for you. Or I wish I was the father that rested your infant head in my palm, supported your spine in the crook of my arm and then let you sleep near my heartbeat. I should have done that for you too. I won't insult your intelligence by saying I wasn't able, I just didn't.

Now here's where I need to be honest with you and with myself about relinquishment. They never asked me to relinquish you. There must have been something in your file because I thought I saw one nurse look at me through the nursery glass, then go check something in your file. After that she didn't pick you up and bring you closer to the glass for me to get a better look like she did for the other fathers. Instead, she left the nursery, walked past me down the hall without looking at me, and came back with a social worker.

The social worker then took me aside and asked if I was marrying the mother. I immediately, without hesitation, said "No". They took the two decisions to be one and the same: Marry the girl, keep the child; don't marry and lose the child. There was no such thing as fathers' rights back then.

Then she asked me something curious, whether I was an Indian. I answered truthfully because she seemed to already have it in her file. I think she *tsked-tsked* and either wrote a margin note or crossed something out. I saw that. My mind reels at the thought that only a few years later the Indian Child Welfare Act would have made it automatic for that social worker that Rémy and I get to keep you.

On the other hand, I didn't fight for you. I have had to live with that. My passivity was only part fear. Another part was opportunism or a way to escape the complications of having my soon-to-be wife raise the daughter that resulted from my affair. It wasn't about you personally; you were a baby. You weren't rejected. Better put, the rejection I made was of the situation and of my responsibility, but not of you.

It's true that we visited two abortionists. One was on Riverside Drive here in Manhattan. The other was over the George Washington Bridge in Fort Lee, New Jersey.

As I told you over brunch, it's true that I am pro-choice. Not to terminate the pregnancy was a choice. You were a choice, Faith. After giving it more thought, I don't even think your conception was entirely an accident. Even before it was made legally available in the 1970s, everyone who'd served in the army like I had knew about prophylactics. Ophelia had been around the block, too. I've already said I'm not really a religious man. But let me slip into that language and say maybe you were meant to be. It would be inappropriate to say more than that to a young lady.

You are quite an accomplished young lady! A profile on NBC's Sunday Today show for being the first American producer in Japanese television. Three healthy kids by your early thirties. I was finally able to locate the women's magazine with your cover story. It wasn't at the newsstand but I bought a copy at a bookseller. I always wanted you to have a good life and it looks like you've found that. You've made that with the opportunities your adoptive parents provided.

I'm curious as to how those pictures turned out that you took of me. I should have flagged the waitress to have her take one of us together. I don't think I cracked a smile. I didn't feel I had the right. I wasn't there for you over the years. I'm what they call a deadbeat—that's what was running through my mind when you snapped those pictures. That, and I'm considered fairly intense, frowning when I think I'm looking relaxed, tight-lipped when I think I'm smiling. Cameras catch me out.

I'm actually the luckiest guy in the world. Not only did you turn out okay, we found each other and you wanted to meet me. Faith, you're kinder than I deserve. You must be a wonderful mother, I doubt the kindness you've shown me is exclusive. I think it shines on anyone lucky enough to be near you.

Please give him, your father, my profound thanks.

I don't know what his and my relationship would be, if any. I want him to know that since that affair I went on to marry the woman I said I would. I've supported her and the son I kept. I've paid all my taxes, my bills, thanked people who've helped me along the way. I've tried to live my life right since then. Maybe even a little because of you, Faith.

You mentioned hearing from Ophelia's sister that your maternal grandmother thought she'd seen you on the Lexington Avenue bus. I remember I'd met them both briefly. I was either dropping Ophelia off or picking her up on the Rosh Hashanah and Yom Kippur holidays when I met them. Ophelia's sister Janice was a bird, like a Jewish Audrey Hepburn. Her mother was petite too with almond eyes. Ophelia's have that same angle tilting up at her cheekbones, but not as round.

I thought about you saying you grew up near a lake. I enjoyed hearing about you going down with a friend and putting on skates while sitting on a log. Pushing off onto wide, black ice. I'm glad you had that growing up. That's one thing your mother and I did during the brief months together. We went to Rockefeller Center and skated there under the giant golden statue of Atlas. There was also a top floor indoor rink, closed long ago, in another part of the city that we went to twice where you could see the whole city around you and both the Hudson and East Rivers. You'd like that. That's something all three of us share.

I didn't finish addressing your surprise at my having gone into the field of adoption. In some ways it's a logical progression. As you guessed, it's no coincidence. In all honesty, it was my way of trying to right a wrong: just as you said, I spend my waking hours writing checks to adoptive parents and foster parents who, like yours, are raising another person's child as their own.

I regret deeply, agonizingly, that I wasn't there any time you needed a dad and am glad you had another dad. Being a dad to Kieran has been very important to me. I still can't quite cobble that together with my not being there for you. I'll own it: I wasn't at your graduations, your wedding, or to meet you at the airport after you came back from England and visiting Ophelia.

Fathers, as Franz Kafka wrote in his 'Letter to My Father,' should at least be there to welcome their children.

* * *

Faith feels lighter. It is all there. The birth of the true. The end of the lies and the hiding, a kind of Heaven, if only they could have had it on Earth. That was a loss that is for keeps. Then she thinks of that song she and Susan had fallen into once. The quiet original Aztec Camera version of "Birth of the True" and not the raucous cover by the Tony Silvio Project. It runs through her head like the soundtrack at the end of something longform.

The singer croons that sometimes he's down, not because of you, but because of "that sense of the impossible, gratuitously handed down." A few more verses, the guitar accompaniment fades, and then Faith sings the last lines like a blessing "on every whisper that welcomes the inconceivable/And the birth of the true."

Faith folds the letter.

READING CLUB DISCUSSION 1: SOUNDTRACK FOR THE DOCUMENTARY

Instead of the usual reading club list of questions, we offer you a list of songs that Faith and Ryuji might use for the documentary. Some tunes are about relinquishment or reunion. Some songs are performed by adoptees or birth-parents. Some are part of the emotional landscape of the stories of ROCK MEMOIR, *From a Desert City by the Sea*, and *Finding Faith*. As you go through this list, remember, guess, and discuss.

1. 867-5309/Jenny (Tommy Tutone)
2. Beechwood 4-5789 (The Marvelettes)
3. Birth of The True (Aztec Camera)
4. Birth of the True (Roddy Frame)
5. Blackbird (Crosby, Stills & Nash cover of Beatles)
6. Century City (Tom Petty)
7. Cinderella (Firefall)
8. Empty Pages (Traffic)
9. First Cut Is the Deepest, The (Cat Stevens demo tape)
10. First Cut Is the Deepest, The (Sheryl Crow)
11. How Sweet It Is/To Be Loved by You (James Taylor)
12. Humble and Kind (Tim McGraw)
13. Little Green (Joni Mitchell)
14. Lovechild (Dianna Ross & The Supremes)

15. Mandolin Wind (Rod Stewart)

16. March 14th (Drake)

17. Melissa (Allman Brothers)

18. Mercy Is (Patti Smith & Kronos Quartet)

19. Mother & Child Reunion (Paul Simon)

20. Never Comin Down (Keith Urban, Melissa's favorite song)

21. Not Fade Away (Buddy Holly)

22. Not Fade Away (Rolling Stones with Brian Jones)

23. Ophelia (Robbie Robertson/The Band)

24. Pennsylvania 6-5000 (Glenn Miller Band)

25. Perfect Day (Chris Whitley)

26. Perfect Day (Lou Reed)

27. Sister Golden Hair (America)

28. Story of Adidon, The (Pusha T)

29. Wake Up Little Susie (The Everley Bros.)

30. Walk This Way (Steven Tyler & RunDMC)

31. Walking in Memphis (Marc Cohen)

32. Whistling Past the Graveyard (Screamin' Jay Hawkins)

33. Won't Get Fooled Again (The Who)

Faith created this game as she, Susan, and others waited in the shadow of the statue of the Goddess of Justice. How would you answer these questions? Would you check both Absurdity and Redemption for some? Are there any that have no answer? Discuss.

1. Having to be grateful for something Faith was told doesn't matter and she should forget.
This is:
( ) Absurdity
( ) Redemption

2. It is legal to marry your biological mother, brother, sister, or father, if you're an adoptee or DCP, but not genetic strangers if they are close legal relatives.
This is:
( ) Absurdity
( ) Redemption

3. As an aggressive, thick-skinned member of the NYC press corps, Faith still thought it was 'inappropriate' to

ask questions about her origins.
This is:
( ) Absurdity
( ) Redemption

4. Some people who want children can't have them and other people who can have them don't want them.
This is:
( ) Absurdity
( ) Redemption

5. The trope that adoption is supposed to 'save' Faith and contrast it to the reality of her birth-father's being willing and able to raise her.
This is:
( ) Absurdity
( ) Redemption

6. Faith thinks 'I didn't deserve that' when she thinks of the early travel to Japan she got to experience, thanks to her maternal adoptive grandfather's generosity, or the college education paid for by her adoptive father, or the fact that the agency placed her with an interesting mother she loved.
This is:
( ) Absurdity
( ) Redemption

7. Faith had to pay a third party to learn her personal heritage. Who pays someone to learn their own mother's

name?
This is:
( ) Absurdity
( ) Redemption

8. Faith remembers being told she was 'not really Jew-ish' because her adoptive mother was Christian and then it turns out her maternal blood great-uncle was the Chief Rabbi for the British Empire.
This is:
( ) Absurdity
( ) Redemption

9. Faith learns about her Cherokee, Choctaw and Mo-hawk ancestry only to hear THAT SAME STUFF; she's 'not really Native'.
This is:
( ) Absurdity
( ) Redemption

10. Both of Faith's ethnicities, Indigenous Americans and Jews, are each only two-percent of the population of the USA and worry existentially about their numbers while simultaneously turning away some adoptees and DCPs with Indigenous or Jewish heritage.
This is:
( ) Absurdity
( ) Redemption

11. Some unwed mothers gave their infants away out

of shame for having them and then years later decline to have them back out of shame for giving them away.
This is:
( ) Absurdity
( ) Redemption

12. The man who gave away his first born and then his next daughter went on to work in the field of adoption and fostercare for the City of New York.
This is:
( ) Absurdity
( ) Redemption

13. It's not unusual for the ancestor-less adoptee or their spouse to become the family genealogist, not only because they've gotten good at reunioncraft but because they feel called to it.
This is:
( ) Absurdity
( ) Redemption

14. Just when scared or control-freaky people turn to anonymous and no-contact donors, donor-conceived people discover adoptee allies and DNA tests.
This is:
( ) Absurdity
( ) Redemption

15. The adoption agency that once sealed away Faith's Indigenous heritage has also testified in the lower courts

in this case *in favor* of heritage equality.
This is:
( ) Absurdity
( ) Redemption

ACKNOWLEDGEMENTS

The backstory of Black, Jewish, and Latino war heroes being recognized belatedly with the US Congressional Medal of Honor is true. The character of Master Sergeant Solomon Leonard Morris, US Army (Ret) is inspired by them and by my adoptive cousin, C. Albert Feissner, and my birth-uncle, Roger Gilbert, who served at Yokota Air Force Base and Misawa Air Force Base respectively.

My appreciation to my beta readers, Elaine Durbach, Fred Firestone, the late Lynn C. Franklin of Lynn C. Franklin Associates, Ltd., International Literary Agency, Patricia Knight Meyer (who is finishing the commitment to being a beta reader made by her late birth-father, Jerry Knight), Traci Onders, Ridghaus, Kara Rubenstein-Deyerin, and Alesia Weiss but most especially to Mark A. Furman, for being my alpha and omega to boot.

Finding Faith has benefited indirectly from conversations with these writers: Toi Derricotte; Meg Kearney; Tim Mayo; Betty Jean Lifton; and, Martha Woodroof, as well as Chris Bauer; Austin Camacho; Michelle Cameron; Jamie Freveletti; Diana Drew Greyson; Jenny Milchman; Mira Peck; Susan Wiedman Schneider; and, Kate St. Vincent Vogl.

This quest has been a companionable one because of the genetic genealogy support of Blaine T. Bettinger, Richard Hill, CeCe Moore, and Demi Morgan, as well as the encouragement from fellow travelers, including Cassandra Adams, Amanda Baden, Sangita Benbow, Ty Cliffel, Rich & Treasure Cohen with the Lubetkins, April Dinwoodie, Rabbi Renee Edelman, Jennifer Dyan Ghoston, Jonathan, Kristen & Mary Gilbert, Fred Greenman & Barbara Raymond, Hal Grotevant, Pam & Suke Hasegawa, Ann Heffron, Emily Hipchen, Bert Hirsch, Susan Ito, Marcie Keithley, Bruce Kellogg, Samuel & Carolyn Kriegman, Michelle Madden, Tom McGee, Joni Mantell, Pat O'Brien, Joyce Maguire Pavao, Samuel Pitkowsky, Marci Purcell, Lynn Riker, Pamela Roberts, Barbara Robertson, Reverend Lynn Rubier-Capron, Carol Schaefer, Rod Shinners, Kathleen Walz, Dana Woods Fried, and Naoko Yamane. In the passages about Melissa, I am especially grateful to Lisa Levine Pfeffer, Jon Messer, and Ross Klein Tabisel. For legal insight I am beholden happily to Leslie Chang, Esq. and Lisa Plaut, Esq.

About The Author

Michele Kriegman, was born, relinquished, and adopted in New York City. She graduated from Wellesley College and received a Japanese Ministry of Education graduate scholarship to Sophia University's Department of Mass Communications in Tokyo. There she began a journalism career at ABC News, followed by multi-year assignments with Nippon TV's top-rated morning show, among others, and was a producer on a Gabriel Award-winning documentary on Peace Studies in Boston and Hiroshima.

Having worked in a second career as a cybersecurity professional for over fifteen years, Michele now devotes herself to writing full time, focusing on two genres: cybercrime mysteries, and search and reunion novels. Her 2014 debut novel, *Tapioca Fire*, written under her birth-name Suzanne Gilbert, is the prequel to *The Birth-Fathers' Club Series*: *ROCK MEMOIR*, *From a Desert City by the Sea*, and *Finding Faith*. She speaks as keynote, panelist, and presenter on both technology and child welfare topics.